金衣人历险记

—— 徘徊在艺术与生活之间的哲学故事

（中英文对照本）

『美』理查德·舒斯特曼 著

陆 扬 译

THE ADVENTURES OF THE MAN IN GOLD

PATHS BETWEEN ART AND LIFE
A PHILOSOPHICAL TALE

Richard Shusterman

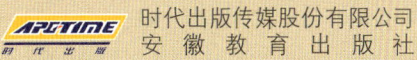

时代出版传媒股份有限公司
安徽教育出版社

图书在版编目(CIP)数据

金衣人历险记:徘徊在艺术与生活之间的哲学故事 / (美)理查德·舒斯特曼著;陆扬译.—合肥:安徽教育出版社,2019

ISBN 978-7-5336-8966-7

Ⅰ.①金… Ⅱ.①理…②陆… Ⅲ.①行为艺术-艺术哲学-通俗读物 Ⅳ.①J198-02

中国版本图书馆 CIP 数据核字(2019)第 260905 号

金衣人历险记:徘徊在艺术与生活之间的哲学故事
JINYIREN LIXIANJI:PAIHUAI ZAI YISHU YU SHENGHUO ZHIJIAN DE ZHEXUE GUSHI

出 版 人:费世平
质量总监:何换生
策划编辑:王竞芬
责任编辑:王竞芬 徐 宇
装帧设计:何宇清
责任印制:陈善军

出版发行:时代出版传媒股份有限公司 安徽教育出版社
地　　址:合肥市经开区繁华大道西路 398 号 邮编:230601
网　　址:http://www.ahep.com.cn
营销电话:(0551)63683012,63683013
排　　版:安徽时代华印出版服务有限责任公司
印　　刷:安徽新华印刷股份有限公司

开　本:710×1010　1/16
印　张:9.25
字　数:120 千字
版　次:2020 年 5 月第 1 版　2020 年 5 月第 1 次印刷
定　价:56.00 元

(如发现印装质量问题,影响阅读,请与本社营销部联系调换)

舒斯特曼的《小王子》梦

——译者序

这个标题有点突兀。理查德·舒斯特曼是美国实用主义哲学的领军人物，他同《小王子》这个70多年来家喻户晓的童话故事又有什么干系？不过我其实在做一篇命题作文，命题的不是别人，就是舒斯特曼这位当今世界上极具盛名的身体美学家。事情得从日前复旦大学召开的身体美学研讨会说起。舒斯特曼是这场少长咸集、群贤毕至盛会的主宾，发言的主题是介绍他最近一部新作——《金衣人历险记》（*The Adventures of The Man in Gold*）。这书标题让我们想起《汤姆历险记》《哈克历险记》《丁丁历险记》。"金衣人"又是何许人也？看大家一头雾水，舒斯特曼开始侃侃而谈，逐一释疑，直至云开雾散，众人始恍然大悟。哲学家的行为艺术，以及这经历反过来引发的返璞归真哲学思考，始露真容。

说起来，金衣人已经8岁了。据舒斯特曼郑重其事交代，他出生在2010年的一个夏日，地点是巴黎近郊的洛雅蒙（Royaumont）修道院。这个地点是舒斯特曼后来一直引为自豪的。当年，法国的修道院漫山遍野、多不胜数。但是像洛雅蒙这样位于湖畔的皇家修道院，历经近千年沧桑完好保存下来的，究竟是屈指可数。细数起来，路易九世是它的父亲，路易十三和黎塞留是它的常客，大革命之后，虽一度变身棉纺厂和女修道院，然终而在1960年为洛雅蒙基金收购，成为驰名国际的文化中心。不仅如此，洛雅蒙还是大巴黎地区迄今保存最为完好的西都会（Cistercian）修道院。西都会是中世纪最森严的苦修主义教派，视世间一切荣华为过眼云烟，西都会修道院唯供僧侣们青灯孤影，冥想上帝。上帝也许不会想到，舒斯特曼说，欧洲大陆哲学和英美哲学的第一次联席会议，就是在这个古老修道院里召开的。

就在2010年的一个夏日，舒斯特曼告诉读者，他与他的法国朋友，灯光艺术家扬·托马（Yann Toma）在洛雅蒙不期而遇。扬照例摆出相机和灯光设施，有意给自称为游牧哲学家的舒斯特曼拍摄行为艺术照片。不过这一次的经历有点特别。对此舒斯特曼本人的描述是，"我原本想穿自己的衣服拍照，可是扬别具匠心。他拖了一个塑料袋，拎出两件金光闪闪的紧身衣，叫我穿进去。他解释说，那是1970年的演出服，是他爹妈的，他们是巴黎国家芭蕾舞团的明星呢。"就这样，当时舒斯特曼这位年届六十的哲学家，硬着头皮钻进了昔年青春靓丽芭蕾舞演员的紧身衣。他倒希望穿不进去来着，宁可半途而废。可是没料想恰好合身。黑漆漆的厢房里，配合灯光，摆拍过几个姿势之后，舒斯特曼发现紧身衣内的自我开始变异。他不复满足于听人摆布，渴望同哲学家本人一样来闯荡大千世界。就在次日午后，洛雅蒙的周末午餐上，闪亮登场的舒斯特曼博得女主人一声惊呼：L'homme en Or（金衣人）！作为哲学家舒斯特曼的另一个身份，金衣人就此诞生。

《金衣人历险记》中有篇后来添补的序言，是为金衣人从巴黎到纽约，后来又到丹麦一路历险的一个哲学说明。序言说，这部图文并茂的历险记，交织着一位西方哲学家细致入微的流水叙事，还有金衣人本人非同寻常的天国视角，更有中国道家哲学的无名玄妙。尤其是这个近似走火入魔的故事，除了身体美学的实践层面之必须，还涉及作者本人2009年的婚姻变故。

书中这样描述了这段经历：

> 那是一个浪漫的下午，夕阳西下，我迷人的女伴坦率地告诉我（兴许是想进一步诱惑我吧），虽然她崇拜我的美学胜过当代任何一种其他学问，但是这学说当中缺了一样最是紧要的东西：艺术家的视角。她说得很对，我的理论就像大多数艺术哲学，完全是在听凭观察者或者说阐释者的观点摆布。倘若把艺术家的经验也包括进来，我的美学会更臻完美。想想尼采对康德非功利静观传统的尖刻攻击吧（它跟皮格马利翁的放纵投入式美学构成多么鲜明的对照），我承认她说得有理。我问她，但是我如何建立艺术家的视角呢，既然我的艺术训练是一片空白？她调皮地眨了眨杏眼，递给我相机，解开白衬衣，仰面躺在床上，酥胸半露。"给我拍几张照片，就这模样，尽情来做艺术家吧。拍完我来给你提意见。要是图片好看，我要让你挑一张最漂亮的，留作纪念，并作为灵感源泉，好来培养艺术家的视角。"我难得摆弄相机，对照相技术基本不通，甚至没来得及调好设置，拍了几个视频片段便草草了事，一张照片都没有留下。她给我指出了那些作品的许多缺点和一些微不足道的优点，然后选了一段，就像她答应的那样，上传到我的电脑里。之后我便把这段视频忘到九霄云外，再也没有看过一眼，直到几个星期之后，我的妻子一如我时常鼓励她的那样，来用我的电脑，偶然发现了这段视频。

> 结果，哲学家原本佳好的第二段婚姻因此终结。两人的女儿跟着舒斯特曼，是哲学家的掌上明珠，如今已芳龄十六。对于他在纽约长大的这位日裔前妻，舒斯特曼显然是心存愧疚。由是观之，金衣人的故事是实用主义哲学走向生活哲学的尝试，身体美学同行为艺术的联姻，同样也不失为哲学家本人生平缺憾的一个补偿。

确认我接下《金衣人历险记》的中文翻译工程，舒斯特曼异常高兴。在复旦光华楼的咖啡厅里，夜色笼罩着巨大的玻璃穹顶，哲学家娓娓谈起了他的小王子梦想，坦言每个成年人都有过小王子的童话经历。小王子长大，就成了安徒生。这也是他2013年访学丹麦奥尔堡大学之际，邀来扬·托马，再度演绎金衣人故事的缘由。而且，为什么上海不能成为金衣人的另一个故乡呢？进而视之，小王子还有另一层含义，舒斯特曼希望他的这部新作，不复是高头讲章、高屋建瓴、高瞻远瞩，反之可以深入到日常生活的阅读层面上去，成为家喻户晓的普及读本，就像当年埃克苏佩里的《小王子》那样。说真的，当今行为艺术竞新斗奇、光怪陆离，可是功成名就的哲学家降尊纡贵，在持续有年的行为艺术里叙写另一种身份认同，在舒斯特曼这部《金衣人历险记》之前，还未见先例呢。

（原载于2017年6月5日《文汇报》）

目 录
CONTENTS

/01/
序 言
PREFACE

/15/
神秘诞生
A MYSTERIOUS BIRTH

/39/
巴黎午夜与热带沙滩
PARISIAN NIGHTS AND TROPICAL BEACHES

/81/
海盗王后的神舟
THE MAGIC VESSELS OF THE VIKING QUEEN

/131/
人物简介
BIOGRAPHIES

/139/
致 谢
ACKNOWLEDGMENTS

序　言

PREFACE

构成本书主干的故事（那本是它的因由所在），似乎是个太为稀奇古怪的混血儿，非事先作一交代，不足以刊行于世。一方面，它提供了千真万确的日期和地点，彼时彼地，我见证了（并且化身为）金衣人的表演。那真是一个不请自来的怪人，他来到这个世界上，全凭我跟巴黎艺术家扬·托马的通力合作。但是另一方面，这个由一位细心的西方哲学家讲述的流水叙事，交织着金衣人本人非同寻常的天国视角，还浸润了道家哲学的无名玄妙。它对事件的观感不但更有诗情画意，而且神秘莫测。这个文本起初不过纯粹是记述我在丹麦奥尔堡同扬·托马的艺术合作过程，或许我们能够将这过程通过艺术展的形式展示出来，连带上我作为丹麦奥尔堡大学访问学者的相关研究。但是金衣人的视角锲而不舍，冷不丁就

The narrative that constitutes the principal text of this book (and indeed its raison d'être) seems too strange a hybrid to make its way without some prefatory explanation. On the one hand, it provides an entirely accurate account of the precise dates and places where I witnessed (and incarnated) the performances of the Man in Gold, an unexpected and bizarre personality who came into existence through my collaboration with the Parisian artist Yann Toma. But combined with this rational chronology composed by a careful occidental philosopher, the narrative presents, on the other hand, the more poetic, even mystical view of these events from the Man in Gold's own eccentric, otherworldly perspective, immersed in the mysteries of Daoism. The text began as an effort to simply record the history of my artistic collaboration with Yann for a possible art show of this work in Aalborg, Denmark, connected with my research as a Visiting Scholar at the university there. But the Man in Gold 's perspective kept insistently

闯入叙述，它的浪漫能量很快反客为主，主导起故事情节的发展，同时不吝遵照凡间的顺序，按部就班地现身于我记录下来的事件里面。

　　这个故事的构思，彰示了它的一个核心主题，那就是自我在走火入魔之后，是多么风雨飘摇、变幻无定。这个主题具有意味深长的美学和身体美学效果：通过金衣人对我身体的占领和转化，我体验到了审美经验的新能力和新途径，同时我也希望，我的读者通过阅读这个故事，同样可以领悟到这些新鲜经验。我开放自己，听凭自己变化多端，也面临着伦理学上的困惑。它有可能导致人丧失自主和自制意识，即便这意识说到底不过是镜花水月，就像金衣人曾经教导我的那样。

intruding itself into the narrative, and its romantic energy soon overwhelmed me, taking control of the storyline while respecting the mundane chronology of the facts I recorded.

The story's composition thus exemplifies one of its key themes: the instability and transformational potential of the self through the powers of possession. This theme has important aesthetic and somaesthetic corollaries: by his inhabiting and transforming my soma, new capacities and avenues of aesthetic experience emerged for me, but also, I hope, for those who follow my work by reading this tale. There are also ethical consequences in opening oneself to possession and transformation; it is risky to lose one's sense of autonomy and self-possession, even if that sense is largely illusory, as the Man in Gold taught me.

我为什么要向这次吉凶莫测的古怪行动开放自身呢?我也不清楚答案。长久以来,我受惠于批判思维的哲学模式教诲,良多感慨生活中的连连惊诧,故而对自知自觉的确定性和洞穿我们真实动机的能力,向来持怀疑态度。我们都是自欺欺人的大师。但是,一旦我试图思考是什么把金衣人带到我身边时,三个因素马上凸显出来,横亘在我鬼迷心窍的道路面前。首先,我经常去形形色色的法国艺术学校讲演身体美学,有时候甚至用身体美学方法来开设实践工作室。在这些场合,不断有人问我一个问题,这问题非常直截了当,而且极其务实,那就是,"身体美学如何应用于当代艺术"。我的回答通常是,身体,以及它的感觉、动量和情感资源,是我们创造和欣赏艺术作品的媒介,所以,身体力行,有助于促生更好的审美

Why did I open myself to this strange possession? I am not certain of the answer. Having long been taught by philosophy's modes of critical thinking and the even more potent surprises of life, I am skeptical of the certitude of self-knowledge and the capacity to penetrate one's true and deepest motivations. We are masters of self-deception. But when I try to understand what brought the Man in Gold to me, three factors stand out as prominent in that path to possession. First was a persistent question I repeatedly faced in the various French art schools where I frequently lectured about somaesthetics and sometimes even gave practical workshops in its methods. The question, strikingly direct and practical in nature, was "how does somaesthetics apply to contemporary art?" My general line of response—that the soma (with its sensory, motor, and affective resources) is the medium through which we both create and appreciate works of art and that therefore improved somatic mastery could generate better aesthetic

经验。可是艺术家们不以为然。他们希望我的理论可以更具体地应用到当代艺术的创作实践上去。我的作品如何提供现成的艺术案例？我也一头雾水。我从哪里去发掘呢？是不是我非得来亲自实践一下？

第二个因素涉及 2009 年 9 月的一段离奇插曲，一开始它似乎无足轻重，但是后来它改变了我的人生。那是一个浪漫的下午，夕阳西下，我迷人的女伴坦率地告诉我（兴许是想进一步诱惑我吧），虽然她崇拜我的美学胜过当代任何一种其他学问，但是这学说当中缺了一样最是紧要的东西：艺术家的视角。她说得很对，我的理论就像大多数艺术哲学，完全是在听凭观察者或者说阐释者的观点摆布。倘若把艺术家的经验也包括进来，我的美学会更臻完美。想想尼采对康德非功利静观传统的尖刻攻击吧（它跟

experience—did not satisfy the artists. They wanted a more concrete and practical application of my theory in contemporary artistic creation. I was at a loss to provide specific artistic examples that emerged directly from my work. Where to find them? Would I have to create them myself?

The second factor involved an odd episode in September 2009 that initially seemed insignificant but proved life-changing. As the sun began to set after a long romantic afternoon, the bewitching woman in my company confessed (perhaps to further enchant me) that though she admired my aesthetics more than any contemporary alternative, there was something it sorely lacked: the artist's perspective. Like most philosophy of art, my theory, she rightly remarked, was totally dominated by the observer's or interpreter's point of view. My aesthetics would be more complete by including also the artist's experience. Remembering Nietzsche's mordant attack of the Kantian tradition of

皮格马利翁的放纵投入式美学构成多么鲜明的对照），我承认她说得有理。我问她，但是我如何建立艺术家的视角呢，既然我的艺术训练经历是一片空白？她调皮地眨了眨杏眼，递给我相机，解开白衬衣，仰面躺在床上，酥胸半露。"给我拍几张照片，就这模样，尽情来做艺术家吧。拍完我来给你提意见。要是图片好看，我要让你挑一张最漂亮的，留作纪念，并作为灵感源泉，好来培养艺术家的视角。"我难得摆弄相机，对照相技术基本不通，甚至没来得及调好设置，拍了几个视频片段便草草了之，一张照片都没有留下。她给我指出了那些作品的许多缺点和一些微不足道的优点，然后选了一段，就像她答应的那样，上传到我的电脑里。之后我便把这段视频忘到九霄云外，再也没有看过一眼，直到几个星期之

disinterested contemplation (contrasted to the passionately engaged aesthetic of Pygmalion), I acknowledged the truth of her critique. But how could I achieve the artist's perspective, I asked, having no artistic training? Her almond eyes sparkled mischievously as she handed me her camera, opened her white shirt and lay back on the bed, her naked chest half-exposed."Take a few shots of me like this; do your artistic best; and I'll then give you instructional critique. If the images are good enough, I'll let you keep the best one as a keepsake and inspiration to go further in adopting the artist's perspective." Inept and inexperienced with cameras, I did not even use the proper settings and ended up taking a few short video clips rather than stills. After reviewing for me their many flaws and meager merits, she selected one and, as promised, uploaded it to my computer where it remained unexamined and forgotten, until my wife accidentally discovered it weeks later when using my computer, as she sometimes did with my encouragement.

后，我的妻子一如我时常鼓励她的那样，来用我的电脑，偶然发现了这段视频。

这段无足轻重的视频一下子变得举足轻重起来。但是它没有开启我作为摄影家的艺术生涯，反倒是开启了我本以为是一段美好姻缘的终结之路。虽然如此，摄影艺术以及它经常是风险重重的摆拍和自我暴露仪式，如今已深深镌刻在我脑海之中。鬼使神差，我发觉这次痛苦的事变也促使我再度不辞风险，来出演金衣人角色。成为摄影家我固然是毫无希望，可是来当摄影模特，做一个行为主体，恐怕我倒是游刃有余呢。

此选择最终通过第三个，也是最为关键的因素，得以生动地展现。我遇到了扬·托马。摄影在他的艺术当中独居高格，他热情

That insignificant photo shoot suddenly assumed immense proportions, but rather than launching my artistic career as a photographer, it marked the beginning of the end of what (I thought) had been a good marriage. The art of photography and its often risky rituals of posing and self-exposure were now, however, very deeply engraved in my consciousness. In some uncanny way, I feel this painful incident prepared me for the risks of posing as the Man in Gold. Although hopeless as a photographer, I might perhaps succeed in the art of photographic modeling as a performing subject.

That option became vividly real through a third, most crucial factor: my encounter with Yann Toma, whose art includes photography as one of its privileged media and whose passionate enthusiasm for collaboration proved irresistible. He was already well acquainted with my writings when I got to know him through my frequent lectures at the Sorbonne's Faculty of Fine Arts (where he was a professor).

洋溢地邀请我合作，我也委实难以拒绝。我是在巴黎大学美术系的讲演上同他相识的（他是该系的教授），在这之前他已经读过我的不少文章。他还跟我拍过一次访谈，那是他在国际哲学研究院(Collège International de Philosophie)一个项目的组成部分，按照规定，举凡被选中出镜的哲学家，必须就他或她著作中的某个核心概念，做一个即兴演讲。我选择了"经验"（experience）一词，这个词在法语中也指实验的意思，使人联想到风险。2009年8月，我们再度在美丽的洛雅蒙中世纪修道院邂逅，彼时我在那里给舞蹈家和舞蹈设计人员开设一个为期三天的身体美学实践研讨班，扬则在给修道院设计一个喷泉。扬知道我的哲学方法是实验的也是身体的方法，心想我也许会乐意试一试他的"能量辐射"

He had also done a filmed interview of me for his project with the Collège International de Philosophie, in which each philosopher selected for filming had to give an impromptu lecture on a key concept central to his or her work. I chose "experience" which in French connotes also a sense of experimentation and associated risk. We met again by chance at the beautiful medieval Royaumont Abbey in August 2009, where I was giving a three-day practical somaesthetics workshop for choreographers and dancers, and Yann was designing a fountain for the cloister. Knowing my approach to philosophy was experimental and somatic, Yann thought I might enjoy experimenting with his photographic art of Flux Radiants, in which he tries to capture and visually represent the energy or aura of a person by tracing it with lights.

（Flux Radiants）艺术，即是说，通过光线追踪，捕捉和呈现某人的能量和灵韵。

那一年8月我为舞蹈的事情忙得不可开交，依然没什么兴趣来当摄影模特。我提议明年夏天再来，到时听凭他调遣。虽然我心底里还是拿不准自己究竟有多大兴趣来履行当时的承诺。不过在这期间，我那位迷人的哲学粉丝导致的诡异的、命中注定的摄影事件，已经改变了我先前对摄影无动于衷的态度。我想，我能不能通过艺术来对已经被我弄得一团糟的人生做出些许补救呢？因此，2010年6月，当我再度来法国做一个系列演讲时，我热切地同扬约定好周末远足洛雅蒙。就在那里，金衣人的故事拉开了帷幕。

Too busy with dance that August and still uninterested in photographic posing, I offered to return the next summer to pose for him, though in my heart I remained unsure of whether I really had the interest to follow through on my offer. In the interim, however, my intriguingly fateful photo shoot with that seductive philosophical admirer had transformed my previous indifference to photography. Could I somehow redeem, through art, the mess I had made of my life? So when June 2010 brought me again to France for a series of lectures, I was eager to meet Yann for a weekend excursion to Royaumont, where the story of the Man in Gold begins.

Yann Toma, Somaflux with Richard Shusterman performing as the Man in Gold: Waiting in the Wings, 2012.
扬·托马,身体流与扮演金衣人的理查德·舒斯特曼:伺机而动,2012。

Yann Toma. Somaflux with Richard Shusterman performing as the Man in Gold; Cabin à Flux. 2012.
扬·托马.身体流与扮演金衣人的理查德·舒斯特曼: 光流小屋. 2012.

我希望读者诸君能充分理解上述交代,因为我无意再提供更多评论。我感觉到金衣人已经迫不及待、跃跃欲试。他即便常常遭人误解,也不耐烦我用干巴巴的、毫无想象力的哲学文章来解说他的行动。他想把他的经历如实地告诉我们,下面我当竭尽所能来帮他述说。虽然我俩心里都清楚明白,对于我们共享的那段经历,文字是多么苍白无力。

I hope the reader is sufficiently prepared to understand it because I feel reluctant to provide further commentary. I sense the Man in Gold impatiently waiting in the wings. Though often misunderstood, he is equally tired of me explaining his actions in my dry, unimaginative philosophical prose. He wants his story told as he lived it, and I have done my best to do so in what follows; although we both know how painfully inadequate it is to the experience we shared.

神秘诞生

A MYSTERIOUS BIRTH

A MYSTERIOUS BIRTH / 神秘诞生

"金衣人"(L'homme en Or)于2010年6月12日周六午后，诞生在洛雅蒙中世纪修道院里。第二天下午，修道院女主人玛丽-克里斯汀·多蒂，给他取了"金衣人"这个名字。当时是在修道院一间私人厢房里，女主人正在举行星期天假日午宴，招待一众亲朋好友，临到收宴，突然发现了他的金色光辉。客人当中包括巴黎艺术家扬·托马和游牧哲学家理查德·舒斯特曼，两人为一项艺术策划一同来到此间。正是这两人，在修道院公共侧厢房的一间暗室里，见证了金衣人的诞生。

倘若说金衣人的出生日期和地点似乎是相当清晰、无可争辩的，他的家系和起源，却始终隐晦不明。金衣人一直不知道他父母是谁。他弄不清楚谁是自己的父亲，不过他倒也不在意这段神秘身世，显然在

L'homme en Or (known in English as "the Man in Gold") was born on the afternoon of Saturday, June 12th, 2010 in the medieval abbey of Royaumont. He was christened the following afternoon by the abbey's proprietress, Marie-Christine Daudy, when she suddenly discovered his golden radiance toward the end of a festive Sunday lunch she was hosting, in the private wing of the abbey, for family and friends. Her guests included the Parisian artist Yann Toma and the nomadic philosopher Richard Shusterman, who together had come to the abbey for an artistic project and who were the sole witnesses of the Man in Gold's birth in a dark chamber of the abbey's institutional wing.

If his date and place of birth seem clear and uncontestable, his genealogy and conception, however, remain shrouded in obscurity. The Man in Gold never knew his parents. He has no clue of who his father might be but does not mind this mystery, apparently regarding even the best of fathers

他看来，即便是最好的父亲，与温柔、幸福亦是了无相干。他更愿意想象自己压根没有父亲。至于他母亲，则又是另外一个故事。他饱含深情地将她勾画为一位舞姿优雅的小小女神，在这里我愿意用中文来表达："舞小星"。她通过一系列诱人的美妙化身，征服了理查德·舒斯特曼的心灵和思想，在那里孕育出金衣人胚胎，直到他长大成人，足够强壮，借助哲学家的身体作为自己的物质表达媒介，终于在一个虽然年已六十却依然不失朝气，自相矛盾地既青春又老迈的身体里，以一条堂堂汉子的身份来到这个世界上。有人认为他是哲学家在梦中受精，自生自长的。哲学家对于他的身份认同，委实是一脸茫然，无从说起。

关于金衣人的身世信息，我就此打住，再无必要深做追究了。他

as benignly irrelevant or blessedly absent. He likes to think he has none. His mother is a different story. He lovingly imagines her as a tiny dancing goddess, Wu Xiaoxing, who through a series of seductive human incarnations captured the heart and mind of Richard Shusterman, and nurtured there the embryonic Man in Gold until he was strong enough to take possession of the philosopher's soma as his material medium for expression, emerging at birth in fully adult form with the body of a youthful sixty-year-old male, paradoxically young and old. Some people believe he gave birth to himself by inseminating the dreams of the philosopher, whose sense of identity he profoundly and quite visibly unsettled.

不会说话。兴许他是从老子那里得到启发,正所谓"知者不言,言者不知①"。倘若有时候他通过理查德·舒斯特曼发表意见,后者也无意将他的思想诉诸文字,而且力不从心。那就尊重这位光辉人物的睿智沉默吧。舒斯特曼敬仰这位大音希声的哲学家,宁可借出自己无言的躯体来给金衣人提供方便,以做肢体交流。那委实比理查德·舒斯特曼,他的哲学代言人搜索枯肠找出的任何词语,更要激动人心而韵味无穷。这也是这本关于金衣人的小书非要配上插图不可的缘故。

有关金衣人的身世,还有一个细节必须交代,那就是他至关重要的助产士,扬·托马。自他出生开始,扬就与他形影相随,成了他的

---

① 引自《道德经》第56章。我使用的是刘殿爵译本 Tao Te Ching(伦敦企鹅出版社,1963)。下同。

There is no point in interrogating the Man in Gold for further information about his origins. He does not utter speech. Perhaps he learned from Laozi: "One who knows does not speak; one who speaks does not know.①" If he sometimes communicates his thoughts through Richard Shusterman, the latter feels both difficulty and reluctance to formulate those thoughts into words. Respecting the wise silence of this shining persona (whom he admires as a philosopher without words), Shusterman prefers to lend his own silent body as the somatic medium for the Man in Gold's gestural communication, which is far more dramatic and potently expressive than any words that Richard Shusterman can muster as his philosophical spokesman. That is why this book about the Man in Gold must be

---

① The quotation is from the *Tao te Ching*, chapter 56. I use the translation of Laozi by D.C. Lau, *Tao Te Ching* (London: Penguin, 1963). Future quotations from this work (hereafter designated as D) will appear parenthetically, also citing chapter number.

保护人。出于一种莫名的直觉,扬意识到有一种神秘的艺术形式在徘徊翱翔,那是围绕舒斯特曼漂泊无定身体的能量灵韵,它迫切渴望在血肉之躯里显现出来。扬是艺术家又是法师,决心将这个胚胎中的小儿,立马变成七尺男儿。他选中了洛雅蒙修道院,因为这里格调高远,风光绮丽,对于一场艺术分娩,正当其地。扬领着对此深信不疑的哲学家,来到他打点停当的产房,排出了一应生产设备:相机、灯光、紧身衣。他的助产士角色居然神差鬼遣,一路延续了下来,因为举凡金衣人现身凡俗,他就必得出场,奉上他那身活力四射的金色肌肤。

目睹了舒斯特曼以他第一人称的权威声音,公开发布这首次诞生的经过,我将在下面的叙述中继续使用第一人称(因为他作为这篇文章的作者,同这个离奇变身故事

illustrated.

One further detail of his origin must be emphasized. The crucial midwife for his birth was Yann Toma, who remains his ever-present companion and protector. With uncanny intuition, Yann sensed a mysterious artistic form hovering as an energetic aura around Shusterman's nomadic soma and yearning to emerge in vivid bodily form. As artist-shaman, he resolved to conjure out this embryonic persona into full personhood. Selecting the Royaumont Abbey as a suitably spiritual and aesthetic venue for this artistic parturition, Yann guided the unsuspecting philosopher to the delivery room he prepared there and provided the birthing equipment: camera, lights, and body suit. His midwife role is mystically unending; for every time the Man in Gold comes to life, Yann must be there to provide his golden, energizing skin.

Witness Shusterman's published testimony about this first birth, using

的当下叙事人，可能同为一人）。

"我原本想穿自己的衣服拍照，可是扬另有主意。他拖出个塑料袋，拎出两件一模一样的金光闪闪的紧身衣，叫我挑一件披挂上身。他解释说，那是20世纪70年代的演出服，是他爸妈的，他们当年可是巴黎国家芭蕾舞团的明星呢。那个周末，我面临的第一个艺术挑战，便是钻进这套紧身衣里去。我心理上的障碍可想而知，要我这60岁哲学家的身体，在这原本是为年轻舞蹈家柔软躯体设计的光闪闪的紧身衣里亮相，鼓鼓囊囊赘肉毕现，委实犯难。更别说如此紧身的尺寸让我活生生钻将进去，也是一种生理挑战。我倒是暗暗巴望这演出服穿不进去，可是我马上看到了扬大喜过望的表情，原来它居然合身。扬容光焕发，帮我拉上背后拉链，大功告成，我变身为后来因此得名的

his first-person authorial voice here, which I will continue to use in what follows. (For he, the author of that essay, may be identified with the present teller of this curious tale of transfigured identities). "I was expecting to be photographed in my own clothes, but Yann had other ideas: he pulled out a plastic bag with a pair of identical glittering gold body stockings and asked me to put one on. They were, he explained, costumes used by his parents who, in the 1970s, had starred in the Paris Opera Ballet. My first artistic challenge of the weekend was getting that garment on. Apart from the psychological barrier of displaying my 60-year-old philosopher's figure in a glitzy skin-tight body stocking that had been designed for lithe young dancers and that revealed every bulge in my soma, there was also the physical challenge of actually getting into its very snug dimensions. I was half hoping the body stocking would not fit, but then very glad to see how happy Yann was that it did. He beamed as he helped me close

'金衣人'。倘若说中世纪以降，炼金术师们孜孜不倦地寻找'哲人石'以点铁成金，那么毋宁说在这个中世纪修道院里，炼金术的一种后现代形式业已闪亮登场。扬将一个稀松平常的中年哲学家，变成了一件金光闪闪的艺术作品，即便很难期望会有人来崇拜它的美丽。"①

扬摄影风格的形成由来已久，它源自达达主义奠基人曼·雷的空间书写。这是一种用光线来画画的艺术形式，从词源上看，它正呼应了"摄影"（photography）这个词的最初意义。为完成这样一件摄影作品，扬要求他的模特在完全黑暗的空间里保持完全静止的状态，为便于把握，这个空间通常是在室

---

① 见：理查德·舒斯特曼．黑暗与光明中的哲学家//安妮－玛丽·倪娜科，编．明晰：内视觉，2011.我对原始文本有所补充，突出了扬父母亲的舞蹈背景。

the zipper on the back, completing my transfiguration into the 'Man in Gold', as I would later be dubbed. If alchemists since the Middle Ages have sought the legendary philosopher's stone that allegedly could transmute base metal into gold, then in this mediaeval Abbey a postmodern form of alchemy was at work, with Yann transforming an ordinary middle-aged philosopher into a golden work of art, albeit one unlikely to be admired for its beauty."①

Yann had been working in a photographic style that derives from Man Ray's space writing. It is a form of drawing with light (which echoes the etymological origins of "photography"). To perform this photographic work, Yann has the person pose totally still in a totally

---

① See: Richard Shusterman. *A Philosopher in Darkness and in Light*. Anne-Marie Ninacs (ed.). *Lucidité. Vues de l'intérieur/Lucidity. Inward Views* Le Mois de la Photo àMontréal, 2011: 280—288. I amend the original text to specify the dance background of Yann's parents.

Yann Toma. Somaflux with Richard Shusterman performing as the Man in Gold: Portrait of the Man in Gold. 2010.
扬·托马.身体流与扮演金衣人的理查德·舒斯特曼:金衣人肖像.2010.

内，但有时也在夜间室外。他将相机固定在三脚架上，调节成长时间曝光模式，镜头对准拍摄对象。扬本人为求隐身效果通常身穿黑衣，手提着一架摄影灯，他按下快门，走近拍摄对象来细细感受其灵韵，用灯光来追踪它。而这灯光，刹那间围绕对象身体，金蛇狂舞。扬必须移动迅速，这不仅是为捕捉人物流动不拘、变幻无定的能量灵韵，也为了确保只是将静止的人物姿态和光线踪迹，而不是艺术家的身体或灯具，抓拍到胶片上面。这般突如其来的一阵狂舞之后（持续时间取决于他的感觉，不过我的体验是，通常不超过一分钟），扬回到三脚架边，关闭镜头。然后他稍作歇息，准备再度出击。这样拍出来的照片，拜扬那盏手提摄影灯的轨迹所赐，勾画出摆拍对象披金戴银的奇幻光线，

dark setting, typically indoors for better control but sometimes outside at night. After positioning his camera on a tripod, adjusting it to a special setting for the long exposure, and aiming it at the photographic subject, Yann (typically dressed in dark clothes to make himself less visible and holding a hand lamp) releases the camera shutter and then approaches the posed subject in order to better sense its aura and trace it with the lamp's light, which energetically whirls around the subject's soma. Yann needs to move swiftly, not only to catch the moving, changing flow of the person's auratic energy but also to ensure that only the stationary posing subject and the tracing of the lights (but not the artist's body or lamp) will be captured on film. After a burst of such energetic swirling (whose duration depends on what he feels but, in my experience, usually lasts less than a minute), Yann returns to the tripod and closes the shot. He then catches his breath for another sortie. The photographic

Yann Toma.Somaflux with Richard Shusterman performing as the Man in Gold: Dreaming Soma. 2010.
扬·托马.身体流与扮演金衣人的理查德·舒斯特曼:梦想身体.2010.

Yann Toma. Somaflux with Richard Shusterman performing as the Man in Gold: Darsonvalisation. 2010.
扬•托马.身体流与扮演金衣人的理查德•舒斯特曼：达松伐电疗. 2010.

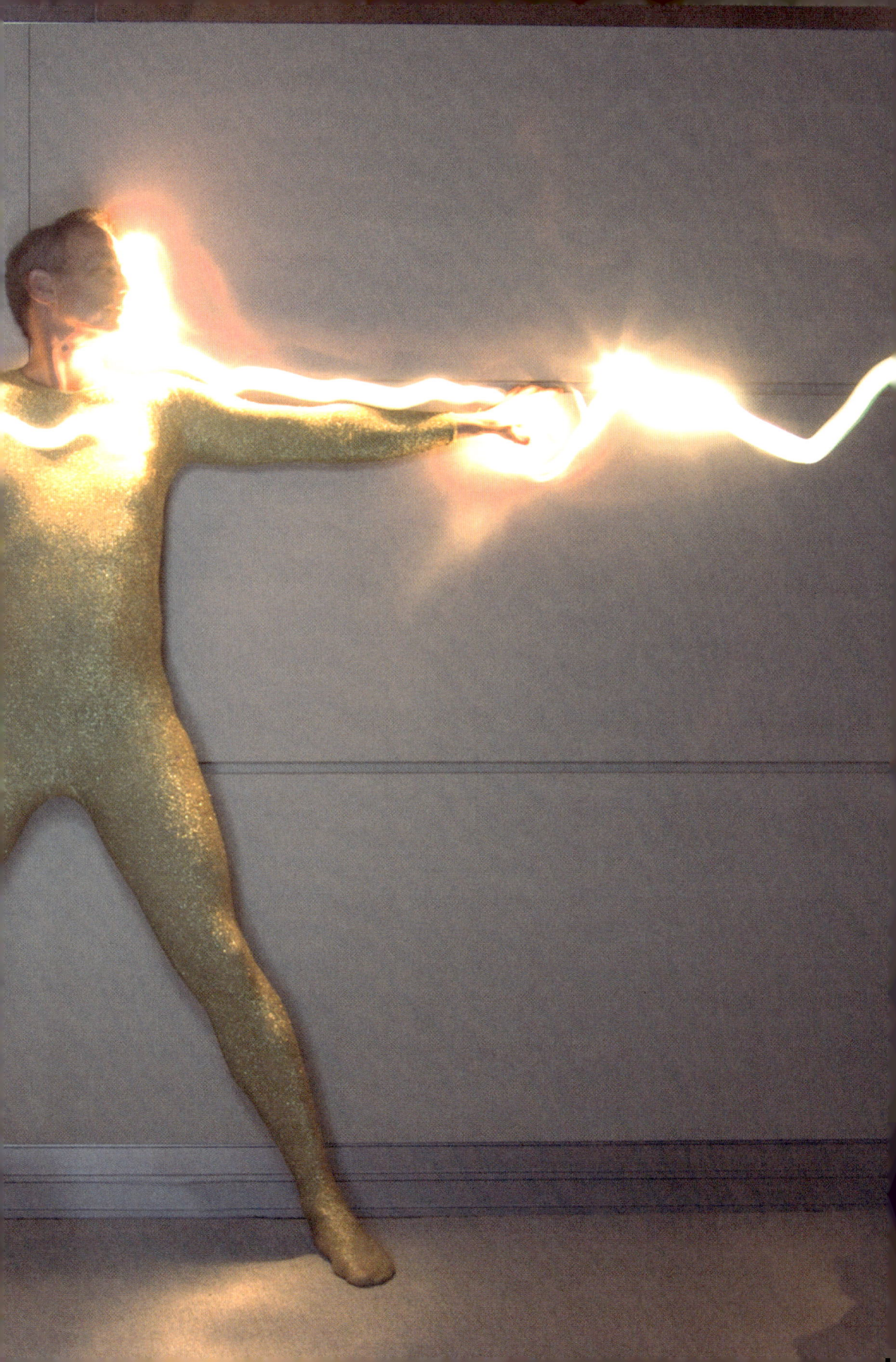

将他从对象身上感觉到的目不可见之灵韵,以视觉形象表现出来。①

作为拍摄对象,扬给我的指令是摆出各种姿态,就在修道院那间黑漆漆的厢房里保持绝对的静止状态,不但一动不动,而且不许说话。我们悄无声息地忙乎了一个下午,直到黄昏,才偃旗息鼓,得以同我们的修道院主人一道悠闲地用餐。夜半过后,我们再度披挂上阵,又折腾了三个小时。我累得不行,无奈只能偷懒,半卧半躺变换姿势,迷迷糊糊半睡半醒,恍恍惚惚之间,似乎总能感觉到扬专心致志在我横卧在地的金色身体上方忙碌不休。也许正是在这些神志恍惚的时刻,金衣人自己的意识在扬的生动灯光

image that emerges portrays the posing subject surrounded by the lines of light created by the trajectory of Yann's hand-held moving lamps, rendering visible the invisible aura he senses in the subject.①

My instructions as Yann's subject were to remain perfectly still in the various poses I took in the dark Abbey chamber. My imposed motionlessness included my mouth. We worked silently and long through the afternoon and into early evening, when we shed our equipment to dine leisurely with our Abbey hosts. After midnight we resumed our work for another three hours; my growing fatigue inspired a series of reclining poses in which I drifted in and out of sleep, always somehow aware of Yann's attentive movements above my reposing,

---

① 在我的《通过身体思考:身体美学文集》(Cambridge: Cambridge University Press, 2012)"作为行为过程的摄影"一章中,我对扬·托马这一技术的方法和谱系有更为详细的介绍。

---

① I provide more details on the methods and genealogy of Yann Toma's technique in the chapter "Photography as Performative Process". in: Richard Shusterman. *Thinking through the Body: Essays in Somaesthetics.* Cambridge: Cambridge University Press, 2012: 239—261.

的刺激下，开始苏醒过来。

　　星期天上午晚些时候，我们重整旗鼓，准备在摄影房里开始第三场操练。6月的修道院阳光明媚，我穿过百花争艳、芬芳可人的庭院，想起又要在那个阴暗地牢里一动不动地摆姿势，禁不住哆嗦了一下。一旦进入室内，我规规矩矩套上了衣服，可是当扬给我那身光闪闪的肌肤背后拉上拉链，拉到最后几厘米时，我突然心有所动，又哆嗦了一下。摆了几小时姿势后，我忍无可忍，再也不甘心如一潭死水般静止不动。某种内在的力量蠢蠢欲动，终于喷薄而出，那是一种不可抑制的能量。它要出去，它渴望光明。扬建议我们喘口气，歇一会。可是我按捺不住心里一阵悸动，破门而出，一路跑过长廊，越过台阶，追踪着诱人的花香，来到庭院里，那正是鲜花盛开的6月，花团锦簇，

goldclad body as I fluttered in and out of consciousness. Perhaps in those moments of lost consciousness, the Man in Gold's own consciousness was coming to the fore, stimulated by Yann's dynamic light.

Late Sunday morning we returned for our third session in the shooting chamber. Crossing the Abbey's courtyard, which was radiant with sun and fragrant with myriad June blossoms, I shivered at the thought of another long session of posing in the cold, grim dungeon of immobile darkness. Once inside I dutifully donned my costume, but felt a strange inner tug when Yann zipped up the last few centimeters of its tight, shining skin, as if something inside me bristled at my confinement. After a few hours of posing, I could no longer stay motionless. Some inner force compelled me to quiver and shake with irrepressible energy. It wanted out; it wanted light. Yann suggested we pause and rest. But possessed by an irresistible burst of movement, I shot through the chamber door, running

绿草如茵。扬一把抓起摄像机, 紧随着奔了出来, 仿佛他的魔法师直觉早就预见到了此情此景的戏剧性变化。待我到得花园里, 我已不复明了自己在干什么。更确切地说, 我已经不复是我了。

花园里鸟语花香, 阳光和煦, 生机勃勃。我迷失了自我, 金衣人反客为主, 支配了我。他开始自行其是, 他的自我意识羽翼既丰, 便开始自得其乐, 摆出他的大丈夫独立性来。他不复听命我那具学院派身体的许多羸弱陋习, 不复甘心听凭扬的摆布, 一动不动待在暗室里做模特。正相反, 他要闯进大千世界, 不但在夜里, 而且在光天白日之下; 且让扬委屈一下, 来追踪他的历险轨迹吧。记得舞小星吗, 那位舞姿翩翩的小女神, 金衣人对她无比崇敬, 把她看作母亲和圣洁爱人, 她不但激发了金衣人的身体美

down the long corridor and steps leading out to the courtyard, following a seductive scent to the Abbey's enchanting gardens in full June bloom. Yann grabbed his movie camera and dashed after me, as if his shamanistic intuition had foreseen this dramatic change of pace and venue. By the time I reached the garden, I no longer knew what I was doing. More precisely, I was no longer I.

In the flowering garden, rich in fragrance, sun, and movement, I lost my sense of self as the Man in Gold possessed me, absorbing for himself the full light of self-consciousness and expressing his manly will of independence. No longer would he submit to the humdrum habitus of my academic soma; no longer would he limit himself to posing motionless by following instructions for Yann's photographic stills in darkness. Rather, he would roam free in broad daylight as well as night, while Yann instead would follow his lead to trace his adventures. Channeling the spirit of Wu Xiaoxing, the tiny dancing

A MYSTERIOUS BIRTH 神秘诞生

Yann Toma. Somaflux with Richard Shusterman performing as the Man in Gold: Photographic still from the film *Chateau*. 2010.
扬·托马．身体流与扮演金衣人的理查德·舒斯特曼：电影《城堡》剧照．2010.

学思想和激情，而且使舒斯特曼的艺术变形记梦想成真。凭借舞小星的精神引导，金衣人开始在花园里翩翩起舞。他因地制宜，就地取材，自编自导他的舞蹈剧。他跳过树篱，跪在地上，闻最细小花儿的芬芳，忽而又从池塘里掬一钵清水，洗去脸面手心的汗液。待到信心倍增，他走到修道院大门口，同一大车瞠目结舌的游客面面相觑。最终是扬把他喊了回来，扬还没忘记已答应了同修道院主人一家和朋友共进午餐。

时间太紧了，加上我心不在焉，懒得去那黑屋子里拿回哲学家的衣服，于是金衣人同扬直接就去了修道院里的私人公寓，会合正在露台上午餐的客人。这群人眼见扬领来一个闪闪发光的怪人，大吃一惊。这位幽灵般的不速之客，同样是惊慌失措，窘迫万分。他满脸通红，

goddess whom he reveres as his mother and as the divine lover who inspired Shusterman's somaesthetic thought and passion (thus enabling his artistic transformation), the Man in Gold began to dance around the garden. Inventing choreographic narratives based on the venue's affordances and energies, he leaped over shrubs, knelt to smell the tiniest of flowers, and refreshed his sweating face and hands with water from the pond. Gaining confidence, he approached the Abbey's entrance gate where he exchanged curious looks with a busload of visiting tourists, before Yann called him back, remembering the commitment for Sunday lunch with the Abbey owner's family and friends.

Too late and too distracted to recuperate the philosopher's clothes from the shooting room, Yann and the Man in Gold returned directly to the Abbey's private apartments to join the guests lunching on the terrace. The company was astonished to see the strangely shimmering figure that Yann brought to the table; the unexpected apparition himself seemed equally

A MYSTERIOUS BIRTH
神秘诞生

Yann Toma. Somaflux with Richard Shusterman performing as the Man in Gold: Photographic still from the film *Chateau*. 2010.
扬·托马.身体流与扮演金衣人的理查德·舒斯特曼：电影《城堡》剧照. 2010.

跟金色的肌肤适成对照。好在修道院女主人玛丽-克里斯汀见多识广、善解人意，她明白他并不完全是理查德·舒斯特曼，是以亲切招呼眼前这位手足无措的社交新手，管他叫"金衣人"，又把他热情地介绍给了姐姐和女儿，她们好像挺高兴同他拥抱。金衣人社交初获成功，更为这热情鼓舞，决心跑出修道院的高墙，到外面的世界去闯荡一番。于是乎午餐之后，扬带着金衣人踏上了修道院周围的乡间小路。在红罂粟花烂漫怒放的大片田野里，他手舞足蹈、奔腾雀跃，终因兴奋过度，力不自胜，眩晕倒地。

时辰不早，扬该带他回修道院了。他的金衣泥迹斑斑，沾满了荆棘杂草。两人决定下周巴黎再会，找个午夜，舒斯特曼只管睡觉，身体供金衣人化为人形使用。哲学家

shocked and embarrassed: his face was as red as his skin was gold. But the Abbey's wise and wizardly mistress Marie-Christine understood that he was not really Richard Shusterman, so she generously welcomed the embarrassed debutant by dubbing him as "the Man in Gold" and warmly introducing him to her sister and daughter, who seemed happy to embrace him too. Empowered by this social acceptance and energized by its emotional warmth, the Man in Gold sought to explore the world outside the Abbey's walls. So after lunch Yann led him on foot through country roads beyond the Abbey's grounds where he whirled and cavorted in a huge field of red poppies, until he collapsed in intoxicated fatigue from his dizzying frolics.

It was time for Yann to bring him back to the Abbey, his gold suit soiled with mud and studded with prickly thistles. They resolved to meet again in Paris the following week, late one night when Richard Shusterman

Yann Toma. Somaflux with Richard Shusterman performing as the Man in Gold: Poppy fields. 2010.
扬·托马.身体流与扮演金衣人的理查德·舒斯特曼:罂粟花地.2010.

有时候梦见他就是金衣人,可是一旦醒来,又时而纳闷起金衣人是不是也会梦见他就是理查德·舒斯特曼——那位原本过着循规蹈矩生活的学院派哲学家。

should be sleeping and his soma might be available for the Man in Gold's materialization. The philosopher sometimes dreams he is the Man in Gold and, when awake, sometimes wonders whether the Man in Gold ever dreams of being Richard Shusterman, leading the more conventional life of an academic philosopher.

A MYSTERIOUS BIRTH
神秘诞生

Yann Toma. Somaflux with Richard Shusterman performing as the Man in Gold: Bureau du vide. 2012.
扬·托马．身体流与扮演金衣人的理查德·舒斯特曼：空荡荡的办公室．2012．

巴黎午夜与热带海岸

PARISIAN NIGHTS
AND TROPICAL BEACHES

PARISIAN NIGHTS AND TROPICAL BEACHES
巴黎午夜与热带海滩

那一天深夜，就在我乘坐早间航班飞回迈阿密的前夜，扬领着金衣人，开启了他的首度巴黎历险记。他还带来一位才华出众的青年摄影师艾略特·斯托利，以便将他与金衣人的互动拍成电影。扬总是在悉心保护金衣人，为他挡开旁观者咄咄逼人的负能量。他找了一块适宜夜间拍摄的偏僻地方，那是巴黎环线边上，大学城附近的一个边远角落。金衣人不习惯都市的喧嚣交通，却对舞动不息的车灯产生了浓厚兴趣。他爬上邻近的一个广告平台，俯瞰高速公路，这样他能更好地看到车水马龙的景象。他朝它们挥手致意，扬则围着他挥舞自己的摄影灯，艾略特站在高台上，拍下了他们自然而然的手舞足蹈。他们的即兴合作酣畅淋漓，直到凌晨时分，金衣人才从广告平台下来，准备探究沉睡中静悄悄的大学城里的其他

Late in the night before my morning flight back to Miami, Yann took the Man in Gold for his first Parisian adventure, bringing along a talented young cinematographer (Elliot Storey) to film his interaction with the Man in Gold. Always striving to protect the Man in Gold from the negative energy of aggressive onlookers, Yann sought a secluded nocturnal spot, a remote corner of the Cité Universitaire by the Parisian ring-road. Unaccustomed to the noise of city traffic but enchanted by the dancing headlights, the Man in Gold climbed up a nearby advertising platform overlooking the highway so he could better see the rushing stream of cars. He waved to them, while Yann waved his own lights around him, and Elliot filmed the spontaneous choreography of their movements on the elevated stage. Their improvisational collaborative play continued long into the early morning hours, after the Man in Gold descended to probe other corners of the deserted, sleeping Cité. Eager to explore this strange new world, he

Yann Toma. Somaflux with Richard Shusterman performing as the Man in Gold: Photographic still from the film *A night with Richard Shusterman*. 2010.
扬·托马. 身体流与扮演金衣人的理查德·舒斯特曼：电影《跟舒斯特曼的一夜遭际》剧照. 2010.

角落。他急于探索这个奇妙的新世界，小心翼翼地体验自己表演的神奇魔力和力所不及，同时对扬这位忠实的向导和玩伴，这位创意无限的同谋，益发信赖有加。艾略特·斯托利剪辑的电影《跟舒斯特曼的一夜遭际》（*A Night with Richard Shusterman*），记录了他们在巴黎的这第一回表演探索。①

金衣人再度现身，已经是忽忽一年多过去了。我很高兴看到他东山再起，可是也担心我跟他过度紧密的关系，会影响我的哲学家声誉以及家庭生活，甚至，我作为一个遵纪守法公民的立身之本。我的担心缘起于我在纽约拉瓜迪亚机场遭

was carefully testing his powers and limits of performance while developing his trust in Yann as a faithful guide, playful companion, and creative co-conspirator. The film *A night with Richard Shusterman* (edited by Elliot Storey) celebrates that first performative exploration in Paris.①

More than a year elapsed before the Man in Gold resurfaced. I was pleased with his existence but also somewhat worried that my close association with him would prove problematic for my philosophical reputation and my family life, and even for my basic status as a morally decent citizen. This worry arose from a surprising incident in New York's LaGuardia airport less than a month after the Man in Gold's birth. While waiting with my nine-year old

---

① 电影在 Michelle Journiac 画廊的巴黎艺术展《审美转移：艺术与生活中的实用主义哲学》上放映过（2012年5月24日—6月6日），展会详情会展目录（同名发表），以及展会网站 http://aesthetictransactions.webs.com/

① The film was screened at the Paris art show, *Aesthetic Transactions: Pragmatist Philosophy through Art and Life*, Michel Journiac Gallery (May 24–June 6, 2012). For more details on this show, see the exhibitions catalog (published with the same title) and the show's website http://aesthetictransactions.webs.com/

遇的一场意外风波，那时候距离金衣人诞生，还不足一月。当时我跟我9岁的女儿准备登机飞往蒙特利尔，候机时，我们在筛选扬发给我的那些未经整理的电子文件，那都是关于金衣人的洛雅蒙经历的。我们把成功的形象挑选出来，删除掉质量不佳的照片。突然，一个满脸凶相的女安保人员朝我走来，命令我立即关闭笔记本电脑，她说，我在给孩子看色情照片。我解释说，这些照片是艺术，不是色情，可是她压根不听。她还威胁说，倘若我不把这些东西马上删除掉，她就逮捕我。假如连纽约人都以为金衣人在诱发色情，那在更加保守的人群当中，他岂不更是凶险莫测？因为我同他的亲密关系，我自己岂不是也岌岌可危？我有必要强调我自己与金衣人的区别，又不否定同他的亲密关系。因此在以后有关金衣

daughter to board a flight to Montreal, we were sifting through the unedited digital files that Yann had given me of the Man in Gold's Royaumont adventures, separating the successful images from those we deleted because of poorer quality. Suddenly a stern-looking female security officer approached me and asked me to close my laptop immediately because, she said, I was exposing a child to pornography. She refused to accept my explanation that the images pertained to art not eroticism, and she threatened to have me arrested if I did not remove them immediately from sight. If the Man in Gold proved provocatively pornographic to people in New York City, how dangerous would he strike more conservative populations? How sinister would I myself seem by my intimate bond with him? I needed to underline the distinction between myself and the Man in Gold, without denying our connection. In all future films of the Man in Gold my name is therefore omitted from the title to indicate that the adventures are those

PARISIAN NIGHTS AND TROPICAL BEACHES
巴黎之夜与热带海岸

45

Yann Toma. Somaflux with Richard Shusterman performing as the Man in Gold:
Photographic still from the film *A night with Richard Shusterman*. 2010.
扬·托马．身体流与扮演金衣人的理查德·舒斯特曼：电影《跟舒斯特曼的一夜遭际》剧照．2010.

人的一切影片里，我的名字都没有出现在片名里，以表明金衣人的故事就是金衣人的故事，哪怕是理查德·舒斯特曼的名字不得不出现在影片前后字幕中的哪一个方位里。金衣人没有身份证，他也没有国籍。他是我们这个星球上的乌有乡公民，某种程度上说，完全可以被看作一个外星人。对于这类外星人身份，我自能感同身受，缘由容我以下再表。

2011年2月，金衣人再度亮相巴黎。我一个星期之前抵达这个城市，在一个身体美学会议上做主题发言。会议上扬介绍了他的金衣人作品，题名为《身体流》。扬坚持请金衣人出山，再来上一回午夜历险。扬深知金衣人喜欢跳舞，所以这一回带他来到巴黎大学的一间艺术工作室，会晤两位美丽的女舞蹈家，她们一样是身着光闪闪紧身

of the Man in Gold, even if the name of Richard Shusterman must appear somewhere in the credits. The Man in Gold has no identity papers; he has no nationality. A citizen of no country on earth, he may be regarded in some sense as extraterrestrial. I can identify with such alien status, for reasons that will later become clear.

In February 2011 the Man in Gold reappeared in Paris the week I arrived to keynote a somaesthetics conference, where Yann presented his work with the Man in Gold under the special title "Somaflux". Yann also insisted on inviting him for another night of adventure. Knowing his love of dance, Yann brought the Man in Gold to a Sorbonne art studio to meet two beautiful female dancers clad in similarly shimmering body suits of silver and blue. There, in utter silence and total darkness (except for Yann's intermittently flickering lamps），they performed a slow improvised dance sequence of interlacing movement and poses through which

PARISIAN NIGHTS AND TROPICAL BEACHES
巴黎之夜与热带海岸

Yann Toma. Somaflux with Richard Shusterman performing as the Man in Gold: Photographic still from the film *Lights in the Dark*. 2011.
扬・托马．身体流与扮演金衣人的理查德・舒斯特曼：电影《黑暗中的光明》剧照．2011.

Yann Toma. Somaflux with Richard Shusterman performing as the Man in Gold. Materialization, 2012.
扬·托马．身体流与扮演金衣人的理查德·舒斯特曼：物化．2012.

衣，一位银色，一位蓝色。就在此间，寂静无声、一团漆黑之中，唯有扬摇曳的灯光时而流过，她们即兴表演，交错互动，彼此摸索着身体和灵韵能量，在扬萨满巫术般的指挥下，缓缓摆出一系列动作和姿势。艾略特也在场，他拍下了这个场景，制作出了影片《黑暗中的光明》。

金衣人折服于扬的引导手势，对两位女舞蹈家的曼妙动作赞叹不已，但是黑暗中他却心事重重——他在想念舞小星，她翩翩起舞的纤细双足、小精灵般的躯体，举手投足娇柔无力，同扬的两位高大舞伴多么不同。这位金衣客人不由得意兴阑珊，无意继续操演。他消失不见，回到了自己的世界。很显然那是一个类似梦乡的世界，因为我偶然匆匆一瞥看到他，那时候我自己在昏昏入梦，梦见美丽的舞小星降身凡尘，那个我深深了解，悉心挚

they explored each other's bodies and auratic energies, under Yann's shamanistic direction. Elliot was there to shoot the episode which generated the film *Lights in the Dark*.

The Man in Gold was touched by Yann's gesture of invitation and by the beauty of the women in movement, but he emerged from the dark with a heavy sadness in his heart—a longing for Wu Xiaoxing whose tiny dancing feet, delicate limbs, and elfin torso were so different from the strong towering figures of Yann's dancers. The golden guest had no taste for a follow-up encounter, and vanished back into his own world, apparently a dream world of some sort, since occasionally I seem to catch a glimpse of him when I find myself dreaming of the beauty of Wu Xiaoxing through her earthly avatars I've known and loved.

In April 2011, I met Yann in Cartagena, Colombia for a Franco-Colombian conference on somaesthetics. Yann

Yann Toma. Somaflux with Richard Shusterman performing as the Man Gold: Space Exploration. 2012.
扬·托马.身体流与扮演金衣人的理查德·舒斯特曼:太空探索.2012.

爱的人啊。

　　2011年4月，我去哥伦比亚的卡塔赫纳，参加一个法国—哥伦比亚身体美学双边会议，又同扬不期而遇。扬从巴黎带来了那套神秘肌肤，希望金衣人穿上它，再度夜间出游，供他拍摄一些照片。扬和其他法国客人住在城里一个普通旅店里，我则被安置在远离尘嚣的海滨豪华酒店。主办人觉得我是美国人，理应受到特殊礼遇。扬想找个安静地方来变他的金衣人戏法，尤其想看看面朝浩瀚大洋和绵绵沙滩，金衣人会是什么反应。夜间11点左右，他带着金衣来到我的酒店。半小时之后，扬昂首阔步走出酒店，直奔沙滩，后面跟着怯生生的金衣人，今天他的金色肌肤外面罩了件普通的外衣，那是他为避免节外生枝，向我借的。万籁俱寂的幽黑沙滩上，他暴露出金光闪闪的肌肤，

brought the magic skin from Paris, hoping to find the Man in Gold to fill it for another nocturnal adventure in photographic performance. While Yann and the other French guests were housed in a modest downtown hotel, I was placed in a luxury hotel on the swanky lido beyond the busy city center because our local hosts presumed that I (as a North American) needed special resort amenities. Seeking a quiet place to conjure up the Man in Gold and eager to see his reaction to the vast ocean and sandy beach, Yann came to my hotel about 11pm with the golden suit. Half an hour later he strolled proudly out of the hotel toward the beach accompanied by the Man in Gold, who shyly followed, his golden skin covered with normal street clothes he borrowed from me so as not to arouse suspicions. In the dark isolation of the beach he exposed his glowing skin to reflect the illumination of the stars of the Southern hemisphere, in whose constellations he could see the dancing figure of his beloved Wu Xiaoxing, mirrored on

辉映在南半球灿烂星空之下。仰望满天星座，他能看到亲爱的舞小星飘逸的舞姿映照在波光粼粼的银色涟漪之上。面对大海，他感到一种深沉的爱，他恍然觉悟，水就是他生命的根本。"上善若水"（《道德经》第8章），他想起了"道"的光辉。

扬结束拍摄，匆匆钻进候在酒店门口的出租车时，已经是凌晨两点多。金衣人大海历险后兴冲冲归来，踏着华尔兹舞步，回到酒店，走进电梯，意犹未尽地套上了我的衣服。可是他的笑容突然僵硬下来，意识到扬忘了帮他拉开金衣后背的拉链。他背过手去，扭成麻花去摸拉链，可是他没法给自己解锁。无奈他只得来到大堂前台。两个壮汉在那里值夜班，一面聊天，一面心不在焉地瞟着电脑里一部日本色情电影。金衣人脱下我的

the softly shimmering ripples of the lightly lapping waves. He felt a deep love for the ocean, suddenly sensing that water was his essential element." Highest good is like water,"(上善若水) he recalled from the classic of the Dao (D8).

It was after 2am when Yann ended the shoot and hurried into a taxi waiting at the hotel entrance. The Man in Gold waltzed into the hotel and entered the lift, elated from his ocean adventure and covered again with my clothes. But his smile suddenly disappeared on realizing that Yann had neglected to unzip his suit. The Man in Gold twisted and turned, flexed and stretched to reach the zipper; but he could not unzip himself, so he returned to the lobby's reception desk where two rugged-looking night personnel were chatting while vaguely gazing at a Japanese porn video on their computer screen."Could you unzip me, please?" asked the Man in Gold politely, removing my shirt to expose his golden suit. The macho hombres stared at him

外套，露出他的金色紧身衣，彬彬有礼地问道："请问能帮我拉一下拉链吗？"这两个彪形大汉紧盯住金衣人，不敢相信自己的眼睛。然后他们窃窃暗笑，满脸鄙夷地交换了几句表示嗤之以鼻的西班牙语。其中一位不屑地耸了耸肩膀，粗暴地一把扯下金衣人的拉链，几乎扯到臀部，说道："好了，太太，还要来个晚安吻别吗？"

金衣人不期遭遇这等粗暴嘲弄，他给吓着了，一溜烟地跑上了楼梯。我意识到金衣人遇到这般人等，所遭致的误解很可能引来暴力虐待，是以次日一早，我找出给扔在一边的金衣，立马退房，带着它去了扬那里。到了晚上，扬连哄带劝，说服犹疑不决的金衣人再度午夜出行，漫步在卡塔赫纳中心城区。他们的起点是索菲特酒店里一个安静的庭院，几个钟点之前，我还同

in disbelief, then derisive disapproval before exchanging some scornful sniggering in Spanish. Shrugging mockingly, one of them harshly tugged down the zipper till it almost reached his golden bottom, uttering "There you go, Senora, do you also want a kiss goodnight?"

Stung by their aggressive taunting, the Man in Gold was also somewhat frightened, and he quickly fled up the stairs. I realized that misunderstanding the kind of man he was could easily lead to violent mistreatment, so early the next morning, when I found the now abandoned golden suit, I immediately checked out of the hotel and brought it to Yann's. By evening Yann had coaxed a hesitant Man in Gold to risk a late-night stroll in Cartagena's city center. They began with the lovely inner courtyard of the Sophitel where Yann and I had dined *al fresco* a few hours earlier with Richard Conte, the Sorbonne professor who was also a featured speaker at the conference. It was a festive Saturday night, and there

Yann Toma. Somaflux with Richard Shusterman performing as the Man in Gold: Sur les ramparts. 2011.
扬·托马．身体流与扮演金衣人的理查德·舒斯特曼：城墙上．2011．

巴黎大学的理查德·孔德（Richard Conte）教授一起在这里用餐来着，他也是会议的主讲人。那是一个周六的夜晚，又值节庆，饭店里依然有几桌饭局未见消歇。金衣人走近第一张饭桌，祝他们用餐愉快，却引来一片惊叫，说是狂欢节已经过去啦，剥掉你那身金皮啊。其他几张饭桌上的人的反应如出一辙，也是恶语相向。金衣人心中惶恐，落荒而逃，扬紧随其后，拍下了这一切。

金衣人沿着熙熙攘攘的街道和广场一路逃窜，一直来到城市边缘的城墙边上。城墙面朝大海，高耸且厚实。他拾级而上，爬将上去，借着探照灯光，举目远眺，仿佛在汪洋大海上搜寻逃生之路。静谧的月光下，轻柔的海浪仿佛软语细声，温存地爱抚着粼粼波光。只可惜没有彩云飞来，带他去往魂牵梦

were still several active dining parties in the restaurant. When the Man in Gold approached the first table to wish them a pleasant meal, he was rebuffed with the cry that Mardi Gras was over and that he should get his costumed butt out of there. Other tables continued the rude commentary, and the Man in Gold bolted in fear, trailed by Yann who tracked it all on camera.

Fleeing from the crowded streets and squares, the Man in Gold reached the city ramparts at the edge of town. He climbed the thick high walls facing the sea, patrolling their elevated paths, peering out with their spotlights, as if looking for an escape into the quiet moonlit sea, whose soft waves spoke with a tenderly caressing rhythm and cast a gentler light. But no cloud came down to carry him to the tranquil home he yearned for; no ship appeared on the water as a horizon of hope. After a few hours of searching for a vessel of redemption, the Man in Gold sadly wended his way back to the hotel with Yann, who sought, unsuccessfully, to

Yann Toma. Somaflux with Richard Shusterman performing as the Man in Gold: Photographic still from the film *Walk the Golden Night*. 2011.
扬·托马．身体流与扮演金衣人的理查德·舒斯特曼：电影《走过金色之夜》剧照．2011.

Yann Toma. Somaflux with Richard Shusterman performing as the Man in Gold: Spanish River Beach. 2012.
扬·托马.身体流与扮演金衣人的理查德·舒斯特曼:西班牙河滩. 2012.

萦的恬静乡，亦不见海面上船只驶过，带来一线希望愿景。可怜一连几个小时，金衣人就这么眼巴巴地搜寻着拯救之舟。未果，沮丧之余，他只能拖着沉重的步履同扬回到酒店。扬一路好言抚慰，告诉金衣人他们这一夜出行，可拍了不少精彩照片呢，却还是白费力气。金衣人陷入了沉思。

在卡塔赫纳，金衣人领略了热带海岸的美，但与此同时，他也明白许多人会把他看作不正常的怪人，因为他搅乱了他们所知的关于一个男人应当外貌如何、举止如何的基本常识。金衣人对自己的男子气深信不疑，知道真正的男人不但具有坚定刚强的"阳"性，同样具有多愁善感的"阴"性。诚如《道德经》所言，"知其雄，守其雌，为天下溪"，（第28章）先贤老子的这段名言，教导他韬光养晦，在卑

console him with encouraging words and artistic images achieved in their nocturnal ramble. The Man in Gold fell deep in thought.

From Cartagena, he learned of his love for tropical, coastal beauty, but also that many would regard him as a deviant alien, disturbing their sense of how a man should look and act. He was confident in his manhood, knowing that true men possess not only hard, yang essence but sensitive yin essence as well, just as real women possess both yin and yang. "Know the male but keep to the role of the female and be a valley" (D28), （知其雄，守其雌，为天下溪。）advised the legendary Laozi, teaching him to be comfortable in the humble obscurity of low position and gentleness. "The spirit of the valley never dies. This is called the mysterious female. The gateway of the mysterious female is the root of heaven and earth"(D6) . （谷神不死，是谓玄牝，玄牝之门，是谓天地根。）

贱温存中自得其乐。"谷神不死，是谓玄牝，玄牝之门，是谓天地根"（第6章）。金衣人想起了道家的智慧：滋养生命的水汇聚低处，其温柔绵软的"阴"质，可克熊熊"阳"火，劈开最坚硬的岩石。在他炽热的金衣包裹中，他读出了灵魂中"阴"的道理，那是拜天堂里的舞小星所赐。他多么渴望与她嬉水同游啊。

所以难怪，仅仅9个月之后，佛罗里达南部的亚特兰大海岸，时值我在伯克莱顿的身体、心灵与文化中心出席一个会议，与会的扬毫不费力，又找到了金衣人。两人共同度过一个不眠之夜，他们探索海湾中间的水道，从西班牙河漫步到红珊瑚公园，用摄影礼赞身体。除了无所事事的瘾君子疑神疑鬼，时而瞥来一眼，以及扬的一盏灯出了毛病以外，一路都风平浪静。可是

The Man in Gold recalled the Daoist wisdom that life-nourishing water collects in low places and that its soft and supple yin essence can overcome the force of yang fire and cut through the hardest rock. Beneath his fiery gold suit, he recognized the yin principle in his soul, inspired by the heavenly Wu Xiaoxing, and he longed to join her by the water.

Yann therefore had no trouble in finding the Man in Gold along South Florida's Atlantic coast only nine months later, when attending a conference at my Center for Body, Mind, and Culture in Boca Raton. One endless night they explored the intracoastal waterway and roamed the beach from Spanish River to Red Reef Park, celebrating the soma through photography and encountering no stressful obstacles beyond the suspicious squints of lounging potheads and the failure of one of Yann's lamps. But there was also nothing to excite the passions of the Man in Gold, no vessel to convey him

同样也一路平淡，没有什么引发起金衣人的激情，亦无舟楫带他去往希望的港湾。这是一段更适宜宁静沉思，做一做自我分析的时光。金衣人的动因是什么呢？他坐在我住宅附近的一个泻湖码头上，细细思量起来。扬则在一边追踪他的思想能量。我无法用我自己的言辞来描绘他的丰富沉思，即便加上扬的图像也是枉然。我只能在下面的段落里，就我对他的了解，述其荦荦大端。

金衣人背后有两股巨大的推力：爱和恐惧。他朝思暮想他那翩翩起舞的美丽女神，她化身人类，在舒斯特曼这位实用主义哲学家身上播下了种子。虽然也爱凡间的美人，但是他在其哲学生涯的男性祭坛上，无情地牺牲了她们的爱。具有讽刺意味的是，正是她们启发了他的哲学生涯，而且无私地滋养了它。理性论证和巧言善辩，给爱的

to the harbor of his hope. It was a time for more tranquil reflection, for self-analysis. What motivates the Man in Gold? he wondered, as he sat on the dock of a lagoon near my apartment, introspecting while Yann traced his energy of thought. I cannot capture the richness of his reflections in my own words (even if I add Yann's images) but offer in the paragraph that follows the gist of what I understood from him.

The Man in Gold is driven by two great forces: love and fear. He yearns for the beautiful dancing deity whose human manifestations sowed the seeds of his existence in the pragmatist philosopher who loved those mortal beauties but grimly sacrificed their love on the manly altar of his career in philosophy, a career they ironically inspired and unselfishly nourished. To remedy the ruinous damage that reasoned arguments and clever words inflict on love's nurturing power, the Man in Gold eschews discursive language, recognizing it as the glory of philosophy but also an imprisoning

Yann Toma. Somaflux with Richard Shusterman performing as the Man in Gold: Mooring Meditation. 2012.
扬·托马. 身体流与扮演金衣人的理查德·舒斯特曼：水边冥思. 2012.

滋养能力带来了灾难性后果。为补救计，金衣人避开使用论述性语言，他心知肚明那是哲学的光荣，可也是导致了它暴虐愚行——它的片面性的囚牢。所以他宁可在姿势、姿态和行动中来表现自己，以努力赶上轻舞飞扬的美人，它们可都是仙女舞小星的化身啊。金衣人虽然热烈地爱着美丽的舞女，可是这爱里面性的成分却似乎是可有可无的，或者说，他仿佛是通过对情色的高贵化表达，奇迹般地把握了它。他对扬的爱，也缘生并滋长在他们千奇百怪一起舞蹈的方式之中。除了这一类爱，金衣人的动因中还有对知识的爱。那是一种特殊的好奇心，它通过直接的感官经验，接触无以名状的丰富特质来学习，而正是这些特质，在唤醒珍贵的意义，预示深刻的真理。这一好奇心驱使他云游四方，时刻准备接受扬的邀请，

source of its oppressive folly—its one-sidedness. He expresses himself instead in posture, gesture and acture, to emulate the dancing beauties that he loves and learns from, incarnations of the divine Wu Xiaoxing. In his ardor for beautiful dancers the Man in Gold seems indifferent to sex or a magic master of it through ennobling erotic expression. His love of Yann is born and nourished from the ways they dance together. Beyond such love of beauty, the Man in Gold is driven by the love of knowledge, a curiosity to learn through immediate sensuous experience, through direct contact with indescribably rich but nameless qualities that evoke precious meanings and promise profound truths. This curiosity sets him wandering, ever ready to explore the unfamiliar locales and unanticipated situations into which Yann invites him, scenes that Yann himself cannot foresee because their energy is always altered by the entry of the Man in Gold, but not always, unfortunately, in positive or welcoming ways.

前往陌生场域和未知场景，这都是扬本人也始料未及的情景，因为它们的能量总是随着金衣人的进入而变化无定，但是说来沮丧，这种变化并不总是积极的，也并不总是令人舒畅的。

故此，金衣人背后第二股巨大的推力，便是恐惧。和他的爱一样，他的恐惧也是双重的：一是被拒绝的恐惧；一是被误解的恐惧。而误解经常就遭致拒绝。金衣人降生之初固然是受到了热烈欢迎，可是打那之后，他不断受挫，伤痕累累。有人疑神疑鬼，对他不屑一顾；有人怒目以向，将他拒之门外；有人挖苦嘲笑，恶言相斥。这一应尖酸刻薄的闭门羹，让他黯然神伤，落荒而逃。他渴望爱，渴望被人接受。他惧怕这些排斥，只能远远避开社交圈子。即便接受扬的邀请，披挂上阵，金衣人也努力躲避咄咄逼人

Thus, the second great force that animates the Man in Gold is fear. Like his love, it is twofold: fear of rejection and fear of being misunderstood (which often generates rejection). After the warm embrace of his natal coming out, the Man in Gold was repeatedly hurt by the way people snubbed him with suspicion, spurned him with angry looks, rebuffed him with harsh, derisive words that aimed to injure, exclude, and make him flee. Longing for love and acceptance, he dreads such rejections and thus shrinks from social contact. Even when responding to Yann's call by appearing, the Man in Gold will soon disappear into the night, fleeing from the aggressive eyes and scornful words that wound him. He wears those wounds visibly on his golden skin, which though initially seamless and unblemished, now bears a number of small rips and tiny blotches where his adventures have rubbed him the wrong way. (This skin, we should recall, was first designed for the opera stage, not for the ramparts and cobblestones of city walls and

Yann Toma. Somaflux with Richard Shusterman performing as the Man in Gold: Tiandiren. 2012.
扬·托马.身体流与扮演金衣人的理查德·舒斯特曼:天地人.2012.

的眼神和恶言蜚语,很快消失在夜幕里面。他金衣上的伤痕清晰可见,它原本天衣无缝、完美无缺,如今出现不少细小裂缝,也沾染了斑斑污渍。那都是他在历险途中不慎所致。别忘了,金衣当初是为歌剧舞台设计的,可不是为了让人穿着它去爬残垣断壁和卵石城墙,去逛大街。

金衣人惧怕遭人误解,是因为误解不光引来讥嘲白眼,而且出卖和玷污了他的爱,那本是他的希冀和使命,可是误解使之声名狼藉。正是这高贵的爱,让他的金色肌肤散发出光辉灿烂的能量。舞小星凭借她神圣又神奇的炼金术知识,从我的实用主义思想中抽取深藏不露的欲望基因,将之提炼为金灿灿的爱的长生不老药,不但灌入金衣人心扉,而且捶打入他的贴身镀金衣。那一身亮晶晶的好铠甲,包裹同时又激活了他的身体,引导它飞向纯

streets).

The Man in Gold fears being misunderstood, not only because misunderstanding spurs the scorn of rejection but also because it betrays and sullies the love that is his hope and mission. That ennobling love provides the shining energy that radiates from his golden skin. With her divine knowledge of mystic alchemy Wu Xiaoxing extracted the base elements of desire buried in my pragmatist mind and then refined them into a golden elixir of love which she poured into the Man in Gold's heart and also hammered into his finely gilded suit, a shining coat of armor to shape and animate his soma, directing it toward purity of passion. Often, however, the golden skin is misperceived as an outfit of sexual lust and perversion. Short-sighted or small-minded viewers have sometimes even mistaken it for nakedness and thus screamed at the Man in Gold to put some clothes on. Others mistake its snug fit (designed to intensify qi energy) as instead aimed

净无瑕的激情。只可惜,这一身金色肌肤经常被人曲解为性欲和变态装备。有时候遇上近视眼或小心眼的观众,他们甚至误以为那是裸体,因此冲着金衣人尖叫,叫他披上衣服。又有人见它如此贴身(设计原本是要凸显"气"的能量),身体各部位凹凸有致,从而联想到了性交。这些令人痛苦的误解,在纽约便已显而易见,每当他身着光亮金衣,独个儿站着,摆出一个中性姿势,既没有性伙伴或色情工具,也丝毫没有勃起迹象,却被指责说你这鬼模样矗在那里,本身就是色情范本。即便在卡塔赫纳,这个热带风情的消闲胜地,人们依然对他喋喋不休、恶言相对。

也许巴黎,这个光明之城,会给他更多理解和接受,就像他第一夜经历的那样。当年跟她同名的帕里斯以金苹果把美神推举到最高地位,因此名扬天下。这个城市想必

at highlighting those body contours associated with sexual intercourse. Those painful misperceptions were already evident in the New York accusation that the Man in Gold—fully covered by his radiant skin and standing by himself alone in a neutral pose (with no sexual partner or erotic tool or any hint of an erection)—constituted in his own right an instance of pornography. Despite the laidback tropical charm of Cartagena, people addressed him with an equally aggressive tone.

Perhaps Paris, the city of light whose namesake famously prized beauty as the highest deity, would prove more understanding and receptive, as it was in his first night adventure. Thus five months after his South Florida ramble, the Man in Gold emerged again in Paris full of hopeful anticipation. As for me, a distinctive double event required my presence at the end of May. The philosophy and art departments of Paris 1 Panthéon-Sorbonne decided to celebrate the

Yann Toma. Somaflux with Richard Shusterman performing as the Man in Gold: Currents of the Seine. Tiandiren. 2012.
扬·托马. 身体流与扮演金衣人的理查德·舒斯特曼: 塞纳河的水流. 2012.

会给他更多理解和接受，就像他第一夜的经历那样。所以在佛罗里达南部漫游的 5 个月后，金衣人满怀憧憬，再次现身巴黎。至于我自己，5 月底有一个别具一格的双重事件要我参加。先贤祠—索邦那里的巴黎第一大学有意庆祝我的《实用主义美学》出版 20 周年，当年这本书在法国同步出版，书名为《生动的艺术状态》（*L'artà l'état vif*），他们决定召开一个国际会议来讨论它的影响。同时举办的还有一个艺术展，以鲜活生动的形式来展示它的艺术内涵。我应邀来组织艺术展，虽然我在这方面没有任何经验。幸运的是，我可以求助一些艺术家朋友，请他们把作品借给我用作展览。

twentieth anniversary of my book *Pragmatist Aesthetics* (simultaneously published in French as *L'artà l'état vif*) with an international conference on the book's impact, together with an art show designed to present its artistic import in vivid concrete form. I was asked to curate the show, despite my total lack of curatorial experience. Fortunately, I could rely on some artist friends to lend me their works for the show. Yann was one of them; ORLAN, Carsten Höller, Pan Gongkai, and Tatiana Trouvé were among the others. After the exhibition opening[①] and the conference were over, Yann convinced the Man in Gold to join him and Elliot, the filmmaker, for a late Sunday night stroll in the heart of Paris by the left bank of the Seine. The sculptures along the quai fascinated the Man in Gold,

---

① 目击者报道说，展会晚间开幕式上金衣人短暂亮相，然而人群嘈杂、灯光雪亮，很快就吓跑了他。展会网站上可以找到追踪他出场的相关录像。

① Eye witnesses report a brief appearance of the Man in Gold at the exhibition evening opening but the crowd and lights soon frightened him away. A video trace of that appearance can be found on the exhibitions website.

Yann Toma. Somaflux with Richard Shusterman performing as the Man in Gold: Abri. 2012.
扬·托马. 身体流与扮演金衣人的理查德·舒斯特曼: 庇护所. 2012.

扬就是其中之一,此外还有奥尔兰、卡斯顿·荷勒、潘公凯,以及塔蒂安娜·杜薇等。在会议结束、艺术展开幕后①,扬说服金衣人跟着他和制片人艾略特,在巴黎心脏,塞纳河左岸来一次周末午夜巡游。

金衣人迷上了码头边上的一座座雕像,兴致勃勃地扭摆姿势,跟它们逐一嬉戏,塞纳河流水潺潺,游船缓缓上下行驶,络绎不绝,街灯并游船灯光,映照出一片灿烂波光。游船尤其让他心醉神迷,他渴望登上舟楫,以便同河流的一舞一动联姻,与水融合为一体。水,那可是他的神髓啊。

他在那里痴痴幻想,冷不丁河边传来一阵泼皮无赖的粗暴讥嘲声。那是三三两两东倒西歪的醉汉,都是年轻人,手里捏着葡萄酒瓶,指着金衣人捧腹大笑,装作文质彬

who happily posed and played around them, excited by the flowing water with its brightly dancing reflections of street lamps and the lights of tourist boats gliding up and down the river. The boats especially enchanted him; he yearned to board them so he could wed his movement with the river's flow, merge with the water which he felt as his essence.

His reveries, however, were rudely broken by rowdy shouts from roguish jokers who were loitering or sauntering along the riverside. Groups of young men, wine bottles in hand, would point at the Man in Gold and laughingly holler vulgarities in a derisively polite grammatical form."Vous avez une grosse et brillante bite, Monsieur! Je bande pour vous." Guys trying to impress their girlfriends expressed themselves less coarsely in challenging the Man in Gold 's masculinity to heighten their own. "Vous avez une très jolie derrière, Monsieur. Voulez-vous

彬的模样喊着粗话:"您的公鸡大又美哪,先生!我捏一把吧。(Vous avez une grosse et brilliante bite. Monsieur! Je bande pour vous.)"几个小子满心想在女朋友面前争脸,故意咬文嚼字来挑战金衣人的男子气,以显得他们才是真正的男人。

"您的屁股好漂亮喔,先生!我们跳个舞吗?(Vous avez une très jolie derrière, Monsieur. Voulez-vous danser avec moi?)"扬一笑了之,觉得他们大吃一惊之余油嘴滑舌,也是情有可原。可是金衣人对这类污言秽语完全不知所措,只觉得光辉灿烂的爱的愿景,顿时就给人丢进黑漆漆的阴沟里面,藏污纳垢。他狼狈逃窜,在鹅卵石路面上踉踉跄跄,一头撞上了电线杆。扬紧跟其后,努力安慰他,却也是徒劳。他消失了,再也不愿重出江湖。

第二天早上醒来,我浑身疼痛,

danser avec moi?" Yann smiled at their understandable reactions of surprise and jestful mocking. But the Man in Gold did not know how to handle such ribald taunting that thrust his shining vision of love into the dark sewers of sarcastic smut. He fled the scene, stumbling over cobblestones, bumping into pylons. Yann followed but could not console him. He vanished and refused to reappear.

The next morning I awoke aching all over and struggled to get to the airport for my flight to Poland to give a somaesthetics workshop for physiotherapists, fairly convinced that I needed their treatment more than they wanted mine. What sort of healing treatment, I wondered, would be needed to lure the Man in Gold back to our cruel, suspicious world and resume his quest for learning, love, and beauty? Reflecting on his past joys and misadventures I could imagine some key curative elements: an environment rich in natural charms

好不容易赶到机场，飞往波兰，去给一个理疗医师的身体美学工作室做报告。我确信无疑，与其说他们需要我的报告，不如说我更需要他们的理疗。我心里着实纳闷，该用什么样的治疗手段，才能将金衣人拉回我们这个残酷多疑的世界，重新点燃他追求知识、爱和美的热情呢？回顾他往昔的喜怒哀乐，我可以想象出一些疗好他的关键要素，诸如一个满目自然美景、充满人文情感的环境，一块靠近大海的土地，阳光明媚、舟楫往来，甚至还能见到些许雕像。

and human affection, a place by the sea with radiant lights and boats, and even some sculptures.

Yann Toma. Somaflux with Richard Shusterman performing as the Man in Gold: Corona of Concern. 2012.
扬·托马. 身体流与扮演金衣人的理查德·舒斯特曼: 关爱的光环. 2012.

Yann Toma. Somaflux with Richard Shusterman performing as the Man in Gold: Notre-Dame. 2012.
扬·托马．身体流与扮演金衣人的理查德·舒斯特曼：午夜巴黎圣母院．2012．

海盗王后的神舟

THE MAGIC VESSELS OF THE VIKING QUEEN

一年之后，我在丹麦北部发现了这样一个适宜环境。那是2013年，奥尔堡大学请我去做一年访问学者，但是因为丹麦移民法的限制，他们无法向我发出正式邀请。我不是欧洲公民，所以按照丹麦法律，我就是一个不能被合法聘用的外国人。作为一个外国人，想要被合法接受，需要经过一系列非常复杂的官方程序，以及许多生物特征检验，而且必须在官方指定的丹麦境内地点来做。奥尔堡大学对于我的外国人身份也是一筹莫展。我碰了这个钉子，不由得跟金衣人同病相怜，他也深感孤立无援，因为身份异类被拒之门外而倍感沮丧。不过，奥尔堡大学最初邀请我的两位同事——艾尔丝·玛丽·布克达尔和斯达尔·斯坦丝丽温柔化解了我背后的芒刺，给了我非常热情的个人欢迎。她们一起约了一个7月的周末，到艾尔丝·玛丽质朴无

A year later I discovered such an environment at the northern tip of Denmark. The University of Aalborg invited me as a visiting professor in 2013 but was unable to formally execute the appointment because of Danish immigration restrictions. I have no European citizenship, and thus for Danish law I am an alien who cannot be legally employed. To acquire legal acceptance as an alien requires a very complicated bureaucratic process, replete with biometric examinations that must be done in official Danish venues. The university could not find an alternative solution for my alien status. Frustrated by this denial, I felt a special solidarity with the Man in Gold's painful sense of rejection, of being turned away because of his difference. The sting of exclusion, however, was sweetly soothed by the wonderfully warm personal welcome of the colleagues who first invited me to join the University: Else Marie Bukdahl and Stahl Stenslie. Together they arranged a July weekend visit for me at Else Marie's rustic beach

华的海滩屋舍来看我，屋舍矗立在威斯特克里特延绵起伏、裸露着岩石的沙丘上，那正是波罗的海和北海的交汇处，北日德兰半岛的尖端。

我们这次见面的目的是商议奥尔堡大学出版社同意刊行的《身体美学杂志》事项。但是艾尔丝·玛丽，这位丹麦皇家美术学院前院长，同时还想给我们看看两位雕塑家，克劳斯·安托夫特和玛丽特·班蒂·诺尔海姆的工作室。这对贤伉俪住在邻近村庄附近的一栋旧农舍里，周围是良田美景，树木葱茏。克劳斯刚刚完成一尊狮子雕像，打算作为礼物献给丹麦女王。班蒂正沉浸在一个雄心勃勃的计划里，她欲制作一系列规模宏大的维京生命之舟，使用钢筋混凝土材质，表达出一种坚强又优雅的女性主义。所以船首不是常见的龙头，而是一个可爱

house, perched on the rolling, rugged dunes of Vesterklit, on the tip of North Jutland where the Baltic and North seas meet.

The purpose of our meeting was to plan *The Journal of Somaesthetics* that Aalborg University Press agreed to publish. But Else Marie, the former Rector of the Royal Danish Academy of Fine Arts, also wanted to show us the studios of two sculptor friends, Claus Ørntoft and Marit Benthe Norheim, a married couple who lived in an old farmhouse, surrounded by lovely fields and woods, near one of the neighboring villages. Claus had just completed a project of sculpted lions commissioned as a gift for the Queen of Denmark. Benthe was at work on an ambitious project of fashioning a series of large-scale, seaworthy Viking lifeboats made of reinforced concrete and expressing a strong but graceful feminism. Thus, instead of the prow bearing a dragon head, it is crowned with a lovely woman's face while the hull beneath displays her shapely breasts. Else

的女性脸庞，下面船体则勾勒出她起伏有致的乳房。我同艾尔丝、斯达尔在他们的寓所和工作室里度过了一个长长的夏夜。眼见这地方环境迷人、主人好客，特别是艺术能量想象力高张，我心想倘若金衣人重新出山，造访此间，岂不美哉。在此间，他能找到爱和美，还有渴望已久的家园感。在这宁静包容的北欧北方，他可以亮出自己的金色肌肤，打开心扉，而不至于遭人白眼、蒙受屈辱，被撕得片片粉粹。在这里他可以像我一样，远离尘嚣，不再被人当作问题重重的异类而拒之门外。自从 2012 年 5 月巴黎码头那些灾难遭际以来，他再也没有回来过。一年多过去，我和扬都担心他受伤太深，也许就此永远消失。不过我还是心存希望，说服了我的奥尔堡大学同仁们破费安排一次回访，让我带上扬也一起过来。他也

Marie, Stahl, and I spent a very long summer evening at their home and studios. Enchanted by the charming locale, the human warmth, and the imaginative artistic energy, I thought that this could be a place where the Man in Gold might risk a visit. Here he might find the love and beauty and acceptance he so longed for; here in the tranquil, tolerant Nordic north he might reveal his golden skin and open the petals of his heart without their being ripped apart by hostile stares and insults; here he could escape, as I did, the hurt of being rejected as a problematic alien. After the shocks of his May 2012 misadventures on the Paris quais, he had never returned. More than a year had passed; Yann and I worried he would never emerge from the trauma. Still hopeful, I convinced my Aalborg colleagues to invest in arranging a return visit in which I could also bring Yann. He longed to see the Man in Gold again, and I knew the Man in Gold would not take form without him.

期盼良久,希望再次见到金衣人。我很清楚,没有扬在场,金衣人是不肯现身的。

2014 年 5 月 25 日,一个星期天,我跟扬从巴黎假道阿姆斯特丹,飞往奥尔堡,来到艾尔丝·玛丽的海滩雅居,正赶上她准备的美味三文鱼晚餐。我们用法语谈了许多事情,不过中心话题还是金衣人。我们慢慢品着餐后葡萄酒,等待夏日长昼里太阳西下,希望缓缓降临的夜幕终而能请出我们的特殊客人来。我们知道他小心谨慎,断不敢光天化日下贸然登陆北欧。我们望着落日西下,等啊等啊,有些迫不及待。海风呼啸着刮过沙丘,愈见模糊的植被摇曳不止,气温也在剧烈下降。待金衣人到达,已是午夜时分刚过。他无须敲门,我们从窗口望出去,就看到他沿着沙丘间逶迤绵延的小径一路攀援上来。沙丘发端于海边,

On Sunday, May 25th, 2014, Yann and I took our flight from Paris (via Amsterdam) to Aalborg and arrived at Else Marie's beach house in time for the lovely salmon dinner she prepared. We spoke (in French) of many things, but especially of the Man in Gold. We lingered over after-dinner wine and waited for the high summer sun to set, hoping that the growing darkness would finally bring our special guest. We knew he was too cautious to risk his first Nordic landing in daylight. Impatiently we watched and waited, as the sun and temperature dropped and the blustery sea winds shook the dune's darkening vegetation. It was just after midnight when the Man in Gold arrived. He did not need to knock; we saw him from our window, climbing the winding path through the dunes leading from the sea to Else Marie's cabin. Yann and Else Marie eagerly went out to greet him, donning heavy windbreakers to cope with the cold and bringing Yann's camera, lamp, and tripod. The Man in Gold shimmered and trembled; his

Yann Toma. Somaflux with Richard Shusterman performing as the Man in Gold: Sunset in Vesterklit. 2014.
扬·托马. 身体流与扮演金衣人的理查德·舒斯特曼: 维斯克里特落日. 2014.

Yann Toma. Somaflux with Richard Shusterman performing as the Man in Gold: Midnight Fire on the Dunes. 2014.
扬•托马. 身体流与扮演金衣人的理查德•舒斯特曼: 沙丘午夜之火. 2014.

跌宕起伏，一直延伸到艾尔丝·玛丽的小木屋。扬和艾尔丝赶忙出门来招呼他。两人都穿着厚厚的风衣来抵御寒气，扬手里还提着相机、摄影灯和三脚架。金衣人身上闪烁着微光，微微颤抖着。他的肌肤有一股潮湿的海盐味儿，仿佛刚从大海中冒将出来。可是当扬触摸到他，用劲给他拉上最后一寸拉链，激活他颈椎下方大椎穴的时候，说来奇怪，他的身体似乎是全然干爽的。

扬抬头望了望天空，纳闷他的朋友是不是驾祥云而来，而非从汹涌波涛中现身。须知，这两种元素都分享着他至爱的水性气质呢。然后，扬亲吻了金衣人双眼之间的山根，来激活他的"气"，又高举双手，以示祝福，复用他那奇特的萨满腔调咆哮起来："L'homme en Or!"（金衣人！）然后两人开始他们娴熟流畅的摄影舞蹈：金衣人就地一跃，摆

skin smelled moist and salty as if he had emerged from the sea. But when Yann touched him, tugging up the last zippered inch of skin to activate the *da zhui* energy point in the small of his neck, his body seemed strangely dry.

Yann looked up to the heavens, wondering if his friend had arrived by riding the gentle clouds rather than the rough waves (for both elements share his beloved watery essence). Then, kissing the golden guest between the eyes to energize his *qi*, Yann raised his hands in benediction and bellowed (in his special shaman voice) **"L'homme en or!"** Then began their familiar dance of photography: the golden figure leaping to strike a pose and hold it motionless while Yann, after focusing the camera, whirled around him to trace his energy. Spinning from pose to pose, they romped across the dunes. Else Marie watched and shivered, enjoying the collaborative performance but also troubled by the cold wind and worried how the Man in Gold could

出一个姿势,纹丝不动;扬对焦完毕,旋涡般围着他转圈,以追踪他的能量。他们如此这般转出一个又一个不同姿势,嘻嘻哈哈跑遍了沙丘。艾尔丝·玛丽目不转睛、瑟瑟发抖,眼前的合作表演着实精彩,但寒风凛冽,她禁不住担心金衣人那身单衣无法抵挡严寒的侵袭。金衣闪烁着光亮,可是好像没有热量。终于金衣人也身不由己,哆嗦起来,扬这才中止了拍摄。三人回到屋里,赶紧喝一口酒,品一口茶,暖一暖身子。

那一夜金衣人与我同寝。几张慈祥的圣母圣子画像底下,我在狭小的床上开始告诉他明天拜访克劳斯和班蒂的计划,跟他描述他们家里多么温暖、他们的友情多么热诚、他们对艺术又是多么专注。但是他马上打断了我,表示这一切他早有所知,而且他对他们的印象,似乎远比我描述的更有诗情画意呢。

survive it with his skimpy covering. It shined with light but it seemed to radiate no heat. When he began to shiver uncontrollably Yann ended the shoot and they all returned to the cabin to warm themselves with wine and tea.

The Man in Gold slept with me that night. In the narrow bed beneath some comforting Madonna and child images, I began to tell him of the morrow's plan to visit Claus and Benthe, describing their lovely homestead, their warm camaraderie, and their engaging art. But he quickly stopped me, gesturing that he already knew about these things, though his vision of them seemed far more poetic than mine.

Their farm was named Stenshede (meaning "stones on the heath"), but the Man in Gold knew it as the Pink Rock Palace. He realized it was ruled by the Viking Wizard Queen and her husband King of Mighty Stones and Magical Master of the Lions. They had won a great victory for their people.

克劳斯和班蒂的农庄名叫斯坦歇得，意思是"荒原上的石头"，但是金衣人认为它是"粉红岩宫殿"。他知道这里的统治者是海盗女巫王后，以及她丈夫巨石国王和群狮魔法大师。他们为民出征，大获全胜。可是赢得这场辉煌的胜利之后，他们就将宫殿搬到了遥远静谧的北方，不再打打杀杀，而是一头钻进了艺术。他们雕刻有意味的美的形式，而不是兵戈战乱；设计生命和希望的舟楫，而不是死亡之船。这一对皇家夫妻不但有正常的孩子，还创造了两队神奇兵马。国王设计了一队花岗岩狮子，张牙舞爪煞是凶猛，可是又恪尽职守、忠心耿耿，构成一种奇妙的平衡。它们守护着粉红岩宫殿和邻近的工作室，那里可是宝藏无尽呢。要说最美的宝藏，也许是一组惊艳绝伦的女性群雕，她们是王后设计的作品，组成一队

But after their glorious triumph, they withdrew their court to the remote and tranquil North, where they made loving art instead of war: sculpting expressive forms of beauty rather than battlements of destruction, fashioning boats of life and longing rather than vessels of death. Besides their normal children, the royal pair engendered two enchanted cohorts. The King fashioned a troop of granite lions, ferociously strong yet magically balanced by disciplined order and loyalty. They guarded the Pink Rock Palace and its adjacent studios, rich in treasures. Perhaps the most beautiful treasure was the cohort of stunning women that the Queen had fashioned as her troop of disciples: tall, shapely, strongly sculpted but gracefully slender figures, they had unblemished, plaster-white skin and hearts full of life, love, and longing. The Viking Wizard Queen (whose secret name was Blessed Pearl) had endowed them with these gifts which creatively flowed from her own immense powers of passion and allure. Like her radiant smile, these white jade

她的忠实门徒：高大健壮、凹凸有致，可是又娇媚娉婷、楚楚动人。她们洁白的肌肤柔滑如凝脂，内心里充满了对生命和爱的渴望。海盗女巫王后有一个秘密名字叫福珠，她将她自己的无边热情和魅力化为神奇禀赋，赐予了这些雕像。这些洁白的玉女秀色诱人，一如王后灿烂的笑容，势不可挡，她们渴望着冒险和激情。就像她的维京船，她们也满载着王后无边的美和爱。

　　船就矗立在工作室门外，庞大坚固，雪白的船体晶莹剔透。船首是一个制作精美的女性头雕，头雕下方，一对丰满的乳房装饰着船身，一只精雕细刻的女性的手，五指纤纤，优雅地托着乳房。玉女们的期望，全靠这神舟实现了。她们透过工作室窗户凝视着它，急不可耐地盼望出发。王后答应过她们一旦另外两艘舟楫完工——那是她的舰队

maidens were irresistibly seductive and spirited, longing for adventure and affection. Like her Viking ship, they were vessels of the Queen's boundless beauty and love.

The ship stood immediately outside the studio, gigantic and glistening in its pure bright whiteness. A stunning female head crowned its prow, beneath which a pair of lovely breasts adorned the hull, gracefully held by a hand of elegantly sculpted feminine fingers. The ship augured fulfillment of the jade maidens' longings, and they gazed at it from the studio windows with impatient hope and yearning. The Queen had promised to take them on a sailing adventure once she finished building the two other ships necessary to complete her fleet, but their eagerness and curiosity seemed perilously pressing. Innocent and vulnerable, the fair young maidens needed protection. The royal lions were assigned to guard them, not only from attempts to escape beyond the Pink Rock Palace but also from rough

Yann Toma. Somaflux with Richard Shusterman performing as the Man in Gold: Invocation of Love. 2014.
扬·托马. 身体流与扮演金衣人的理查德·舒斯特曼: 爱的祈祷. 2014.

配备所必须的,就带上她们远航大海,闯荡世界。即便如此,她们的焦虑和好奇,依然还是那样动人心魄。这些年轻姑娘天真无瑕、弱不禁风,需要保护。国王的雄狮就是被指派过来守护她们的,不光是怕她们逃出粉红岩宫殿,还得防备外来蟊贼垂涎三尺,觊觎她们的美色。为此王后启用巫术,又加了一道防护,给她们的美艳施上魔法,一旦她们遭遇色迷偷窥,便会立时僵硬,变回雕像,虽然还是艳光四射,却无一星半点色欲诱惑。

在这些倍受珍视的美人中,有一位尤其出类拔萃,她温婉可人、气质绝佳。说真的,她是王后所有美丽创意的理想原型,名叫完美。她那娇小玲珑的身躯是如此迷人,以至于一家日本色情公司找上门来,要买她过去,做生产性爱娃娃的原型。可是她不但美艳无双,而且意

intruders from without who might have lustful designs on their charms. The Queen used her wizardry to fashion a further safeguard for such danger, casting a spell on her beauties such that if they were seen by desiring eyes, they would change their shape and harden into statues, still beautiful in expression but not erotically inspiring.

Among those treasured beauties, one clearly excelled all others in loveliness and spirit. She served indeed as the ideal archetype for all the lovelies the Queen had fashioned. Her name Wanmei (完美) meant "perfect" and her allure was legendary. Her petite but shapely figure was so enticing that a Japanese erotics company tried to buy her to serve as the model for their line of sex dolls. So great was her beauty, so strong was her spirit, that unlike the other maidens, she could maintain her tender charming form if seen or even touched by desiring eyes she did not fear. The Man in Gold yearned to meet her, believing she might prove the long-sought incarnation of the loving

志如钢，不像其他玉女，她即便遭遇色欲目光，也能一如既往，保持温润曼妙的身姿。她不怕淫邪目光。金衣人渴望同她相见，相信她能让他梦想成真：他天长日久期盼着母亲身上那种慈祥的爱能化成肉身，能让他拥抱一下！他在琢磨这信念背后的原委，我却深深堕入了梦乡。

第二天上午我独自苏醒过来，金衣人和我的梦一起消失了。不过我跟扬都确信我们能在斯坦歇得找到他。悠闲地用过姗姗来迟的早餐后，驱车片刻，我们就到了那里。艾尔丝·玛丽把扬介绍给班蒂和克劳斯，后者优雅地欢迎我们，领我们参观了他们的住宅和工作室。我们一边欣赏花岗岩石狮和鬼斧神工的玉女，以及那艘大船，一边告诉主人金衣人也到了日德兰半岛，我们很希望他能够再度现身。社交气氛热情洋溢，就像天气那样，充满

loveliness he saw in his mother but had never held in his arms. As he reviewed the reasons for this faith, I fell into a deep sleep.

The next morning I awoke alone. The Man in Gold had disappeared with my dreams, but I was confident that Yann and I could find him at Stenshede. After a late, leisurely breakfast and a short drive we arrived. Else Marie introduced Yann to Benthe and Claus who graciously welcomed us all with a tour of the house and studios. While visiting the granite lions, the sculpted maidens, and the boat, we told our hosts of the Man in Gold's Jutland arrival and of our hope that he would resurface here. The social vibe was warmly welcoming and energetic, like the weather. The sun shone brightly in a cloudless sky. But that precisely was the problem for the Man in Gold, a creature of obscurity who thrived at night through Yann's conjuring and tracing powers. The lamps that galvanized this golden creation derived their aesthetic energy from the dark. It

了活力。天空万里无云,阳光普照大地。可是这恰恰也成了金衣人的麻烦。他本是黑暗的产儿,唯有夜幕降临,通过扬的神奇追踪魔力,才骤然生动起来。激活这位金色生物的摄影灯,只有在黑夜里方能成就其美学能量。说来也是矛盾,我们在享受美丽阳光,心里却盼着阴云密布、黑夜来临。于是我和扬决定放宽心境,且欣赏周围可人的户外景致吧。我们就在户外享用了一顿漫长的午餐,按照各式各样的丹麦风俗,大快朵颐,猛吃鲱鱼,一杯接一杯地将葡萄酒灌下肚去。午餐后我四仰八叉躺在芬芳如饴的松软草地上,接着享受美味的阳光。很快,我又眼神迷糊,进入了梦乡。

欲望一旦苏醒,何惧黑夜来迟。金衣人来了。他悄无声息地穿过粉红岩宫殿那些空荡荡的房间,找到了扬。扬帮他拉紧拉链,带他走出门外,

was paradoxical to greet the beautiful sunshine with wishes for cloudy gloom, so Yann and I decided to relax and enjoy the lovely outdoor ambiance. After a very long lunch al fresco, where repeated lessons in Danish ways of eating herring were washed down with recurrent rounds of wine, I stretched out on the sweet-smelling soft grass to relax in the delicious sunshine, and I soon dozed off in dreams.

Desire counts more than darkness. The Man in Gold had come and was silently gliding through the vacant rooms of the Pink Rock Palace till he found Yann, who sealed his zippered skin, then whisked him away from the house, eager to find a secluded spot for some Somaflux shots. The Man in Gold rushed straight for the white maidens, but Yann restrained him near the studio door and gestured to the giant Viking boat, immediately adjacent. The Man in Gold assented with a nod, curious to finally discover the insides of such a vessel. They scurried up the long ladder leading to its deck and

迫切地想找一块隐蔽地方,来拍摄金衣人的身体流照片。金衣人冲着洁白玉女直奔过去,但是扬在工作室门口拉住了他,示意他去旁边巨大的海盗船。金衣人点了点头表示同意,不禁好奇这大家伙的里面又是什么模样。他们匆匆攀上长长的悬梯,登上甲板,惊讶地发现它竟是如此绵长宽大。在高高的甲板上举目远眺,美景尽收眼底。但是金衣人的视线很快又转回到王后的工作室,恨不得穿透那几扇窗户。可惜这会儿它们的百叶窗都给拉上了,那本是扬的要求,让屋子黑暗下来,以方便拍照。只不过这制造黑暗的努力显得枉然,午后的太阳光猛烈无比,万丈光芒射向甲板,让人头晕目眩。金衣人本已欲火中烧,发出道道金光,似乎随时会熊熊燃烧起来,抑或耗尽热能,化为乌有。他虽然是光的产儿,但是他属于黑夜,在黑夜中起舞,他方才如鱼得水。

explored the boat's impressive length and breadth. The high deck offered a lovely landscape view, but the Man in Gold quickly turned his gaze back toward the Queen's studio, straining to look through its windows. Yet they were now all covered with shades in an attempt to comply with Yann's request to darken the studio for his photographic work. These darkening efforts, however, were overwhelmed by the puissant afternoon sun, which poured its fiery light onto the boat's dazzling white deck. Already glowing gold and blazing with desire, the Man in Gold seemed ready to burst into flames or melt from heat exhaustion. Though a creature of light, he belonged to the night and felt more comfortable dancing in the dark.

On the boat's bow he found a tiny square hatch leading beneath the deck to the vessel's dark bilge or lower belly: a long, low, narrow, tunnel-like corridor of space directly above the boat's keeled bottom, where unwanted

Yann Toma. Somaflux with Richard Shusterman performing as the Man in Gold: Ship of Longing. 2014.
扬·托马. 身体流与扮演金衣人的理查德·舒斯特曼:希冀之舟. 2014.

在船首，他发现一个四方的舱口，通向船的黝黑舱底，或者说，它的下腹部。嵌有龙骨的船底可以聚集并排出多余的水和其他液体，船底上有一条长长的井道，空间狭小逼仄。他赶紧钻进舱口，想喘一口气，看一看这块奇怪的黑暗空间里究竟有些什么东西。这地方他虽然从没来过，却感到莫名的熟悉亲切，仿佛回到了他美丽母亲的子宫里，幸福地歇息在保护安好的幽暗之中。扬也很高兴终于找到了黑暗，因为他那些个神奇的灯具，唯在此间方能发挥奇特效用。故当金衣人躺倒在排列着根根龙骨的船底上面时，扬的灯光紧跟过来，追踪起他的能量灵韵，期盼这些金色的光线，不仅能将金衣人纯洁的高贵激情表现出来，而且也能打造出一副艺术的盔甲，为他挡开负面能量和无端挑衅。

金衣人歇了一会儿，感觉恢复了精神，便立起身来，使出杂技般

water and other liquids could be collected and removed. He hurried down the hatch to refresh himself and explore its dark strange space, which though still unknown felt uncannily familiar—as if he were back in his beautiful mother's womb, reposing blissfully in protected obscurity. Yann was also delighted with the darkness, for it empowered his lamps to do their photographic magic. So while the Man in Gold reclined on the ribbed bilge floor, Yann's lamps moved over him, tracing his energetic aura with light, hoping these luminous lines would not only make manifest the Man in Gold's purity of noble passion but also serve as artistic armor to shield him from negative energy or aggression.

Feeling rested and reinforced, the Man in Gold arose and acrobatically lifted himself through the hatch and then swung himself over the deck and down the ladder. He slinked surreptitiously around the boat so as not to be discovered, holding himself close to its hull and sometimes pausing to caress,

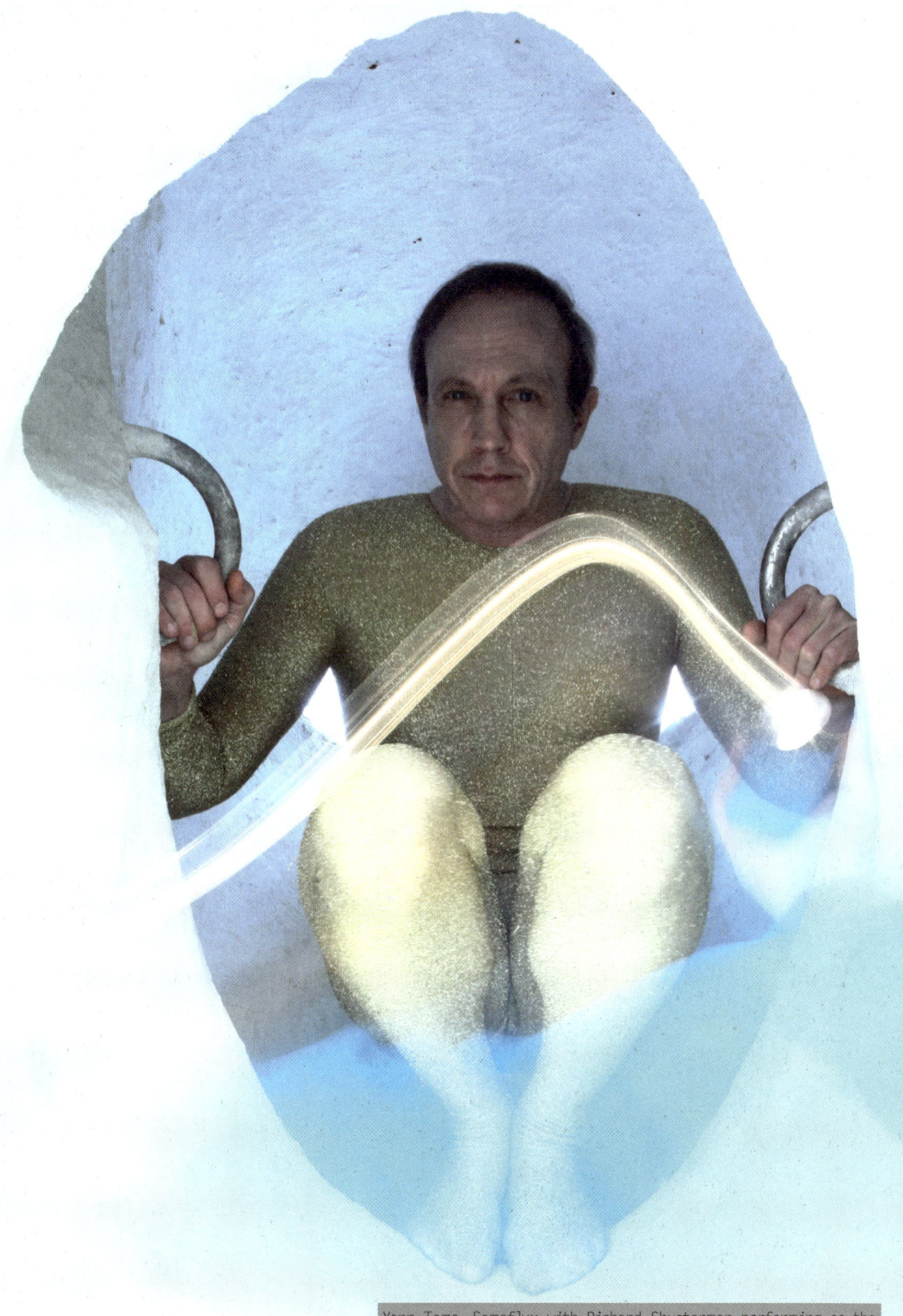

Yann Toma. Somaflux with Richard Shusterman performing as the Man in Gold: Down the Hatch. 2014.
扬·托马.身体流与扮演金衣人的理查德·舒斯特曼:下舱.2014.

Yann Toma. Somaflux with Richard Shusterman perforning as the Man in Gold: Gaze through the Bildge. 2014.
扬·托马．身体流与扮演金衣人的理查德·舒斯特曼：穿过下水道的凝视．2014.

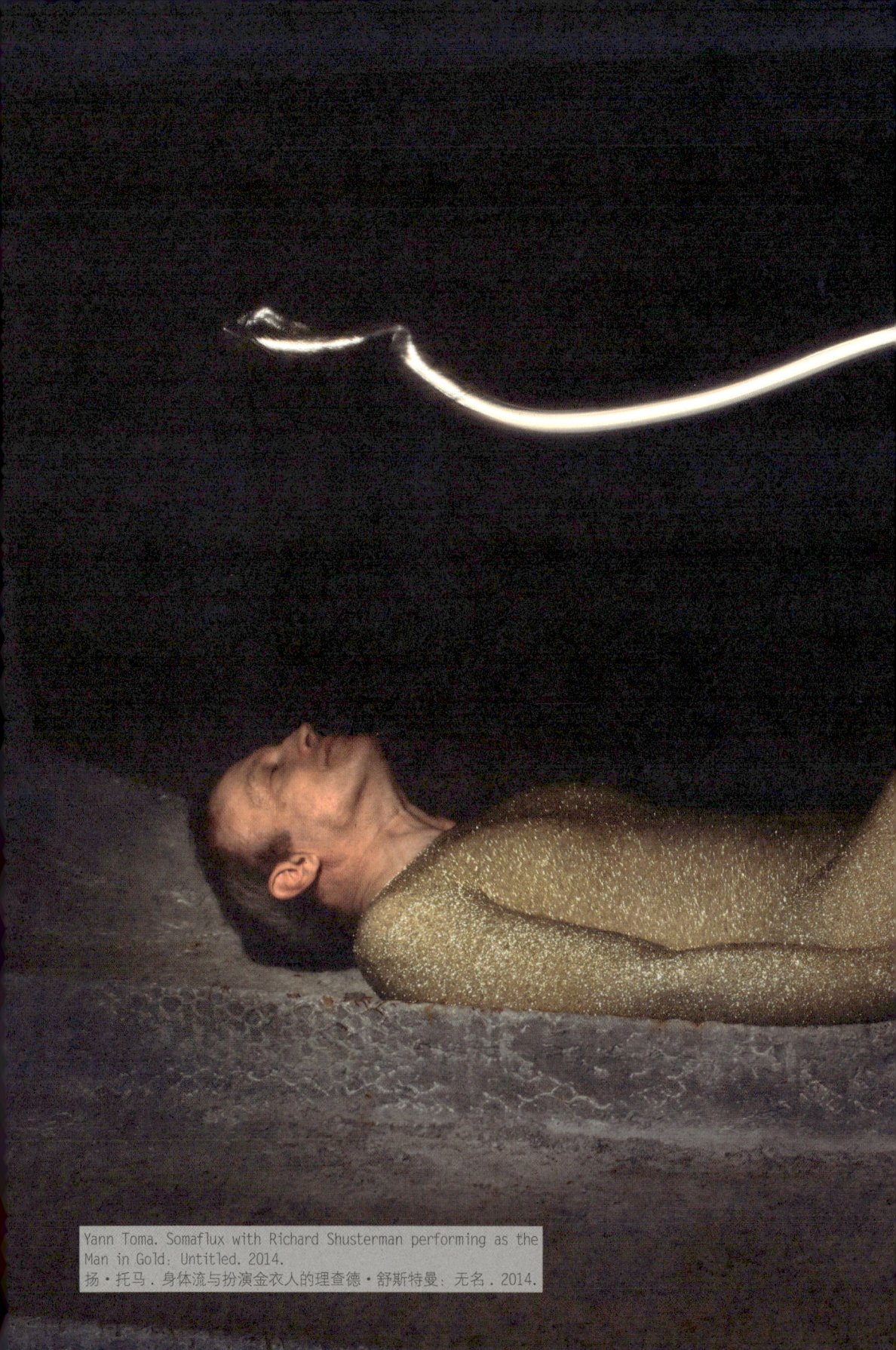

Yann Toma. Somaflux with Richard Shusterman performing as the Man in Gold: Untitled. 2014.
扬•托马.身体流与扮演金衣人的理查德•舒斯特曼:无名.2014.

的好身手，一骨碌蹦出舱口，越过甲板，爬下了悬梯。他静悄悄地绕行船体一周，不想被人发现，时而贴住舟楫外壳，满心虔诚，爱抚亲吻它可爱的女性肢体，他就这样悄无声息地潜行到工作室门口。然后他一步冲进屋内，关上房门，示意扬同他保持距离。在工作室右边，他看到另一艘船只正在建造中，在他左边，有陡峭的木头阶梯，朝上通向洁白玉女们所在的楼层，完美就在灿烂众星之间，惊艳绝伦。但是满屋子高大的女性雕像守着楼梯，那是洁白少女的岗哨，她们站成一个半圆形，如同巨大的亚马逊女战士。金衣人踮起脚尖，小心翼翼地走近她们，架不住好奇，又有点羞怯。她们眼见他走近，却是一声不吭，屹立不动。于是他走近一点，再近一点，可是她们依然毫无动静。这些充满异国情调的雕像居

in reverence and entreaty, its lovely female limbs as he carefully crept toward the studio door. Then, with a burst, he dashed inside and closed the door, signaling to Yann to keep his distance. On the right of the studio he saw another boat under construction, on the left a steep wooden stairway leading up to the floor of the white jade maidens, where Wanmei shined supreme among the galaxy of beauties. But the stairway was guarded by a chamber of giant female figures, the white maiden sentries, standing in a semicircle like colossal Amazons. The Man in Gold approached them warily on tiptoe, fascinated but shy. They remained silent and motionless as he approached them, so he drew closer and still closer but they did not move. Enchanted by these exotic forms towering above him and surrounding him in their circle, the Man in Gold instinctively reached out to reassure them with timid, respectful touches that his intentions were honorable and his affections were pure. Immediately on contact, the stunning sentries stiffened

高临下，包围着金衣人，着实让他心旌摇曳。他情不自禁地伸出手来，想让她们消除疑虑，明白他原出于一片诚心，充满敬意、心怀纯洁地触碰她们。可是刚一接触，这些高大的哨兵立马僵硬下来以示抵抗。她们散发出一种令人陶醉的香气，当时就征服了金衣人，几乎让他一时失明。他闭上眼睛，跟跟跄跄地摸索道路，摸向楼梯，时而抓住个雕像，以作支撑。可是她们自我保护的香气是如此强烈，他人事不省，倒在了地上。

他的柔弱保护了他。霎那间，可怕的女性愤怒转化成了母性慈爱。女哨兵们解除符咒，释放出一阵新鲜香气，唤醒了他。金衣人站起身来，低眉一笑表示感谢，然后再度转身，走向楼梯，心里却想着，完美会如何应对他这位不速之客呢。他刚一举步，耳边突然传来狮

in resistance, exuding an intoxicating fragrant mist that overwhelmed the Man in Gold and seemed to blind him. With closed eyes, he stumbled and groped to find his way toward the staircase, clinging to some of the female forms as pillars of support. But their protective perfume was too strong and he collapsed unconscious on the floor.

His weakness shielded him; the fearful female anger turned to nurturing motherly care. The sentries removed their spell and a new fragrance revived him. The Man in Gold arose and smiled in thanks, then turned again toward the staircase, imagining Wanmei's response to the commotion of his arrival. He got no further than the first step, when he heard the roar of lions. He looked pleadingly at the sculpted sentries but their gaze showed him only one direction of response: to rush immediately out the door and sprint toward the woods beyond the bounds of Stenshede, where he could hide and where the granite lions no

子的吼声。他抬头眼巴巴地瞅着岗哨雕像，可是她们盯住他的目光，全都指向一个方向：让他赶紧冲出门去，逃出斯坦歇得庄园，躲到远处树林里去。惟其如此，石狮的魔法方才无能为力。他在邻近田野里跑啊跑啊，未穿鞋履的脚上沾满泥土和荨麻，他一口气跑进树林里面，耳边再也听不到骇人狮吼。然后他放慢了脚步，喘口气，想找一条小路偷偷溜回到庄园里去。走到国王的工作室附近，金衣人发现一长条花岗岩石板横亘在地面上。石块呈灰斑色彩，就像猛犸象的那种，一端底下垫了一块小石头，微微上翘。这是海盗巨人的床榻吗？还是一个屠杀敌人的祭坛？金衣人摸了摸充满质感的石板，感觉到热浪汹涌而来，那是来自石块的奇迹能量，他身不由己地被吸引过去，把石板当成调理恢复的床铺，容他养精蓄锐，

longer enjoyed their magical powers of movement. He raced through the adjacent fields, his shoeless feet collecting mud and nettles, until he reached a shielding cluster of trees where he could no longer hear the fiercely growling lions. He then walked slowly through the woods, catching his breath and carefully trying to circle his way secretly back to Stenshede. Not far from the King's studio the Man in Gold found a long, rectangular granite slab posed horizontally on the ground. It was speckled gray in color and of mammoth proportions, slightly elevated on one side by a low stone strut. Was it a bed for Viking giants or an altar on which to slaughter enemies? When he touched its textured surface, the Man in Gold felt the hot surge of its magic energy and was irresistibly drawn to it as a bed of healing restoration and fortifying preparation for the nocturnal romance that he envisaged. He stretched himself supine along the slab, enjoying how its sun-warmed surface eased the tensions in his back. The still strong early-evening sunlight

Yann Toma. Somaflux with Richard Shusterman performing as the Man in Gold: Blind Enchantment. 2014.
扬・托马．身体流与扮演金衣人的理查德・舒斯特曼：盲目魔法．2014．

Yann Toma. Somaflux with Richard Shusterman performing as the Man in Gold: Among the Amazons. 2014.
扬·托马．身体流与扮演金衣人的理查德·舒斯特曼：亚马逊女战士包围圈．2014．

准备迎接他神思梦想的浪漫之夜。他仰面平躺在石板上,享受日光烤热的石块给他松弛后背。黄昏的太阳依然热烈,他闭上眼睛,十指交叉按在胸口,以示祈祷感恩。不一会他迷迷糊糊进入了梦境,眼前全是完美的影子,可怜他只是神魂颠倒,到现在还没有真正见过她呢。

　　将近黄昏,我在餐后午睡,被一阵寒意惊醒,那是暮色中的草叶在舔我的肢体。我走进屋子,去见朋友。扬打开了他的笔记本电脑,在向克劳斯和班蒂以及其他几位来访的朋友展示他的作品。很快到了鸡尾酒和晚餐时间。晚餐是在室内进行的,太阳落山,夜风变得冰凉起来。晚餐有自家烘烤的面包、蒜头烤大虾、芹菜土豆和新鲜的德国芦笋,陆陆续续地给端上烛光映照的餐桌来。暮色渐浓,觥筹交错之

made him close his eyes as he joined his palms together on his chest in a gesture of thankful prayer; and he soon dozed into the dusk of dreams, haunted by the image of Wanmei, whom he had never seen beyond his ever present fantasies.

My late-afternoon postprandial siesta ended with a shiver as the chill of the now shaded evening grass licked my limbs. I joined our friends inside where Yann had turned on his laptop to showcase his artwork to Claus and Benthe and some other artist friends who had come to visit. Soon it was time for cocktails and then dinner, which we took inside as the night air cooled with the fading sunlight. Home-baked bread, grilled shrimp in garlic, parsley potatoes, and fresh German *Spargel* arrived at the candle-lit table in endless quantities; conversation and wine flowed freely as the shadows lengthened. Darkness finally arrived as one of the guests took out his guitar and began to entertain us with a series of witty ribald songs he composed in

间，谈兴也益发浓烈。待到夜色终于降临，一位客人拿出吉他犒劳我们，弹起一连串他用丹麦语创作的俚俗民谣。扬原本就听不懂，他心不在焉地听了约莫15分钟，提议允许我们两位先行告退，以便去找金衣人，金衣人在工作室里受了惊吓，之后便消失不见，扬一直在担心他呢。说罢他赶紧收拾相机，径直去了工作室。我则在屋里又驻留片刻，用克劳斯和班蒂的家庭电脑收了几封电邮。

　　金衣人无声无息地跨进海盗王后工作室门槛时，差不多已是午夜了。在朦胧微光中，他满怀敬意，向阴影里的高大岗哨致敬，现在她们似乎也莞尔一笑地欢迎他。他踮起脚尖悄悄上楼，心中"砰砰"跳个不停，努力收敛起迫不及待的欲望，还有恐惧。姣好的完美，不但让他心神向往，而且着实吓住了

Danish. After patiently listening for fifteen incomprehensible minutes, Yann politely proposed that the two of us be temporarily excused from the group so we could look for the Man in Gold, whose studio misadventure and subsequent disappearance still worried Yann. While he hastened to collect his camera and head toward the studio, I lingered inside to check my email on Claus and Benthe's home computer.

It was almost midnight when the Man in Gold slid himself silently inside the Viking Queen's studio door. In the dim twilight he bowed reverently to the tall shadowy sentries who now seemed to greet him with gracious smiles. His heart pounding, he softly tiptoed up the steps, struggling to restrain his impatient desire and his fear. The imagined beauty of Wanmei both pulled and frightened him. He knew (with Rilke) that beauty is the beginning of terror since its overwhelming spell has the power to destroy us. Could he survive the rude rejection of her fleeing from him or her

Yann Toma. Somaflux with Richard Shusterman performing as the Man in Gold: The Lions' Altar. 2014.
扬·托马.身体流与扮演金衣人的理查德·舒斯特曼:狮子祭坛.2014.

他。他跟里尔克一样,知道美是恐惧的开始,因为它排山倒海的魔力,足以摧毁我们。她会漠然无衷,粗暴地将他拒之于门外吗?或者干脆让他离开?要是这样,他承受得了吗?他来到工作室的楼上一层,但见茫茫无边,一切都沐浴在黑暗之中。他睁大眼睛,隐隐约约看到几排洁白的苗条雕像,形状各异、姿态各异,中间隔出一条空荡荡的走道。他没有看见完美。有一瞬间他心沉了下去,可是马上他感觉到了她的存在,即便他还无法看清她的轮廓,甚至对她的方位也还一无所知。她确实没有逃之夭夭,正站在她一群高个子姐妹后面,温文尔雅地观察他呢。她的这几位姐妹靠着房里的中央走道,金衣人此刻就在这里摸索逡巡,他集中目力搜索着黑暗,调动他的全部五官感觉,期望在这些洁白玉女中寻出那位他

sending him away? On reaching the studio's upper level, he found a vast space bathed in darkness. Straining his eyes, he could vaguely discern several long rows of slender white figures, in various forms and poses, along with an empty corridor between them; but he did not see Wanmei. For a second his heart sank in panic, but then he felt her presence though he still could not distinguish her form or even her location. She did not flee but observed him with elegant decorum from behind a cluster of her taller sisters who stood closer to the room's central corridor that the Man in Gold now patrolled, peering intently into the darkness and enlisting all his senses to find among the white jade maidens the one he so ardently wanted, the image he so faithfully sought. Remembering that treasured truth must be shrouded in obscurity, he ritually recited (as if in prayer) Laozi's description of the immortal Dao: "As a thing the way is shadowy and indistinct. Indistinct and shadowy, yet within it is an image.

朝思暮想、魂牵梦萦的人儿。他想到珍贵的真理必包裹在幽暗朦胧之中，仿佛是在祈祷，他认认真真地背诵起了《老子》，老子这样描述不朽的"道"：

> 道之为物，惟恍惟惚。惚兮恍兮，其中有象，恍兮惚兮，其中有物。窈兮冥兮，其中有精，其精甚真。（第21章）

他想把这房间里影影绰绰的人像再仔细地搜索一遍，便来轻轻触摸她们，移动她们的位置，努力向纵深方向看进去，完美就在那里啊。这些少女一经他双手抚摸，马上变成了石头。他感到内疚，好不沮丧。黑暗让他的搜索一无所获，如今仿佛要穿透他的灵魂。他需要光明，给他照亮希望。刹那间，一盏灯亮了起来，扬没有放弃他。就像阴和阳、女人和男人、大地和天空一样，

Shadowy and indistinct, yet within it is a substance. Dim and dark, yet within it is an essence. This essence is quite genuine" (D21).

To search the room's shadowy figures more closely, he gently touched them and shifted their positions, trying to get a better view of the rows further back where Wanmei was hidden. The maidens turned to stone in his hands. He was overcome with guilt and gloom. The darkness that frustrated his search threatened to penetrate his soul. He needed light to give him hope. Suddenly a lamp appeared; Yann did not forsake him. Like *yin* and *yang*, woman and man, earth and heaven, also darkness and light were necessary synergetic complements. As Yann's lights needed darkness to work their magical energy on the Man in Gold, so darkness now required those lights to enable the magical union that Yann's golden companion so deeply desired. Near the end of the corridor, along one of the back rows, he finally found her.

黑暗与光明同样需要协同互补。诚如扬的灯光需要与黑暗协作，以映照出金衣人身上的奇迹能量，眼前的黑暗也需要光明，来使扬的金色伴侣梦想成真，实现如饥似渴的奇妙结合。靠近走道尽头，在那几排幽暗的行列里，他最终找到了她。一如他的想象，她身材不高，娇小玲珑，乳房坚挺。她的裸体姿态自信十足，可是也散发出谦卑的魅力。她为自己那种端庄娴雅的美感到自豪，任由它放射出高雅节制的光彩。这光彩征服了金衣人，他诚惶诚恐，想要溜之大吉，欲行又止，更想径直扑向她身边，终究还是欲行又止。他闭上双眼，回忆如何从脚跟开始呼吸，来平静翻江倒海的心脏。然后他缓缓举步，走向她仿佛相知如故的亲切笑脸，目不转睛地注视着她的美丽。在将她拥入怀中之前，她的美早就征服他啦。但凡"天下

Just as he imagined, she stood small in stature, slim but shapely, with full firm breasts; she bore her naked body with self-assured poise but also charming modesty. Confident yet demure in her beauty, she let it shine forth with elegant restraint. It overwhelmed the Man in Gold. He stifled a frightened urge to flee in awe, then stifled a stronger urge to rush to her side. He closed his eyes, remembering how to breathe from his heels to calm his raging heart; and then he walked in measured steps toward her welcoming, knowing smile, never taking his eyes from the beauty of hers, which already embraced him even before he gathered her in his arms. "In the union of the world," says Laozi, "the female always gets the better of the male by stillness" (D61).

Yann waited discreetly at a distance, granting the lovers a silent spot of privacy to enjoy their blissful moment of eternity alone. But stirred by the beautiful passion he perceived, Yann's

Yann Toma. Somaflux with Richard Shusterman performing as the Man in Gold: Wanmei. 2014.
扬·托马. 身体流与扮演金衣人的理查德·舒斯特曼: 完美. 2014.

之交",老子说,"牝常以静胜牡"。(第61章)

扬小心谨慎地在一边,给这对恋人留出安静的私密空间,让他们享受这欣喜若狂的永恒时刻。可是目睹这绝美的激情,他的艺术家创造欲被激发了,情不自禁蠢蠢欲动起来。他架好三脚架,走近这一对有情人。两人堕入爱河之中,几乎纹丝不动,正紧紧相拥,仿佛在做摆拍姿势,全然不顾扬正举着摄影灯,围着他们跳来跳去,追踪着两人的肢体轮廓和能量波痕。扬眼见这些波痕从两人内心深处发射出来,转瞬就充满了整个房间。拍过几张照片后,扬回过神来,识趣地悄悄退避一旁。他心满意足,他的金衣朋友有情人终成眷属,他的相机也捕捉到了激动人心的时刻和那充满激情的曼妙能量。

artistic libido could not be restrained. He set up the tripod and approached the couple, who were locked in a loving embrace and thus almost as motionless as if they were posing. They paid no attention to Yann as he danced around them with his lamps, tracing the outlines of their limbs and the ripples of energy he felt emanating from their center but encompassing the entire room. After a few shots, Yann recovered his sense of tact and silently withdrew, delighted not only by the joy of his golden friend but by the thrill of capturing that passionate blissful energy on camera.

Yann returned to the house and found me poring over a text on Zhuangzi that had just arrived by email attachment. He beamed as he recounted what he witnessed in the studio, eagerly displaying the digital images on his Canon camera. I had never seen the Man in Gold so firmly poised and confidently present, so happily glowing, and so youthfully

Yann Toma. Somaflux with Richard Shusterman performing as the Man in Gold: The Look of Love. 2014.
扬·托马．身体流与扮演金衣人的理查德·舒斯特曼：爱的表情．2014．

Yann Toma. Somaflux with Richard Shusterman performing as the Man in Gold: La Flamme de l'amour. 2014.
扬·托马.身体流与扮演金衣人的理查德·舒斯特曼：爱的火焰.2014.

扬回到住所，发现我正聚精会神地读一篇论庄子的文章，那是我刚收到的电子邮件附件。他说起方才在工作室里所见，容光焕发，迫不及待地打开他的佳能相机，给我看他拍摄下来的电子图像。我从没见过金衣人如此坚定沉毅、信心满满地出现在照片上，他那美丽爱人的拥抱，把他变得如此神采奕奕、朝气蓬勃。我几乎是要嫉妒他了，因为我自己的浪漫憧憬也油然而生（虽然我深爱的美人，还在千山万水之外）。不过最叫我好奇的，是这对情侣的激情居然将所有的背景光，全都聚焦过来了。通常，扬的光波会在摄影对象轮廓背后留下踪迹。但是这一回金衣人和完美不但没有一丝光线溢出，而且所有的光线似乎都集中到这对有情人身上，仿佛要表达他们相爱拥抱中的激情是如何将所有的光吸引进来的。他

transfigured by the embrace of his beautiful lover. I was almost jealous, as my own romantic yearnings were aroused (yet the beauty that I loved was oceans away). But what most intrigued me was the way the couple's passion focused all the ambient light. Normally the waving of Yann's lamps left traces well beyond his subject's contours. But rather than any lines of light leading out from the Man in Gold and Wanmei, all the luminosity seemed concentrated on the couple itself as if to express the all-absorbing radiance of passion in their loving embrace. The transformative energy of their union reminded me of the mystical sexual alchemy of medieval Chinese erotics, where the older man is taught to drink the medicine of three peaks from his young female lovers in order to magnify his *qi* through which he can recover youthful looks and powers, and even achieve earthly immortality. These medicine-secreting peaks include the mouth, the breasts, and the vagina. But the Man in Gold, as far as we could

们在结合中转化出的能量，使我想起中世纪中国情色小说中的神秘房中术来，年长的男方被教以服用他年轻女伴的舌峰、乳峰、阜峰"三峰药"，以壮气补阳，恢复青春面貌和体力，甚而求得长生不死。但是金衣人如前所见，恰恰相反，是从完美含情脉脉的凝视中，吸收了他的变形营养，这叫人想起柏拉图的观点：眼睛是灵魂的窗户，唯灵魂是生命的源泉，可以不朽永在。也许，两人深情款款、炽热不移的目光交流，激发起了一种更为神圣的不朽精神？他们的身体在强光里燃烧，却没有烧成灰烬。这使人想起另一种不朽神性的神秘标记，那改变了摩西与其族人生活的不朽神性。

我和扬回到晚宴上，兴高采烈地跟大伙儿分享金衣人的好消息，侃侃而谈个中的神秘意义。大家都

see, instead absorbed his transfiguring nourishment from Wanmei's loving gaze, reminding us of Plato's view that the eyes are the windows to the soul, which is our animating source and immortal element. Perhaps the focused intensity and fixity of their wedded gaze invoked a more divine immortality of the spirit? The way their bodies burned with fiery light without being consumed recalled another mysterious symbol of immortal divinity, one that changed the life of Moses and his people.

Yann and I rejoined the dinner party, excited to share the news about the Man in Gold and interpret its mystery and meaning. Everyone wanted to meet and congratulate the happy couple, but when we arrived in the studio, the Man in Gold was gone. It was after 1am when a taxi arrived to bring us back to Else Marie's beach cabin. As we were driving, I glanced out the window and saw what looked like a low, blurry shooting star. Yann saw it too but corrected me. It was simply a

想见一见这对幸福的人儿，送上他们的祝福。可是当我们回到工作室时，金衣人已渺无踪影。等到一辆出租车过来，带我们回艾尔丝·玛丽的海滩屋舍，已经过了凌晨1点。路上，我朝窗外望去，看到低垂的天际模模糊糊有颗流星闪烁。扬也看到了，不过他纠正我说，那是一块发光的祥云，金衣人驾着它升天啦，在那里高贵的爱以崇高能量哺育不朽灵魂，艺术的爱和可爱的艺术家们滋养他成长，金衣人同他们故旧重逢，不亦乐乎。

luminous cloud by which the Man in Gold ascended into heaven to join the immortals, propelled by the elevating energy of ennobling love, nurtured by the love of art and loving artists.

Yann Toma. Somaflux with Richard Shusterman performing as the Man in Gold: Botero Dialogue in Carthagena. 2011.
扬·托马．身体流与扮演金衣人的理查德·舒斯特曼：在卡塔赫纳与波特罗对话．2011．

人物简介

BIOGRAPHIES

理查德·舒斯特曼，佛罗里达亚特兰大大学身体、心灵与文化中心的多萝西·F·施密特杰出人文学者，在牛津大学圣约翰学院获得哲学博士学位。主要著作包括《通过身体思考》《身体意识：静观与身体美学的哲学》《表层与深度》《生活即审美》《实践哲学》，以及《实用主义美学》（已以15种语言形式出版）。他获得的研究基金多不胜数，并分别在中国、丹麦、法国、德国、以色列、意大利和日本担任学术职位。法国政府授予他教育学术骑士勋章，以表彰他的文化贡献。奥尔堡大学授予他荣誉博士学位，表彰他在实用主义和身体美学方面的研究。以他为题的英文和中文研究，已有多种著述面世。2010年起，他投身摄影和行为艺术，同扬·托马合作，创造了金衣人这个人物形象。制片人包威尔·库克

Richard Shusterman is the Dorothy F. Schmidt Eminent Scholar in the Humanities and Director of the Center for Body, Mind, and Culture at Florida Atlantic University. He received his doctorate in philosophy from St. John's College, Oxford University. His major authored books in English include *Thinking through the Body*; *Body Consciousness: A Philosophy of Mindfulness and Somaesthetics*; *Surface and Depth*; *Performing Live*; *Practicing Philosophy*; and *Pragmatist Aesthetics* (now published in fifteen languages). The recipient of numerous research grants, he has held academic appointments in China, Denmark, France, Germany, Israel, Italy, and Japan. The French government honored him as a Chevalier de l'Ordre des Palmes Académiques for his cultural contributions, and the University of Aalborg awarded him an honorary doctorate for his research in pragmatism and somaesthetics. He is the subject of book-length studies published in English and Chinese. Since 2010 he has been working in

津斯基拍过一个纪录片,介绍了舒斯特曼的生平与著作。

扬·托马,艺术家和研究员,在先贤祠—索邦巴黎第一大学获博士学位,并主持该校艺术、创意、理论、美学(ACTE)研究所的艺术与光流实验室。他创建了辐射光流这个艺术门类,由此引导出理查德·舒斯特曼的金衣人行为艺术。托马对光和能量的探索,还包括了观念维度。他接手倒闭的Ouest-Lumière电气公司,将其改造成公司结构的艺术网络,并联手企业家、政治理论家和哲学家,进行艺术研究。他还是联合国的艺术观察家。在2015年12月巴黎气候变化大会上,他划时代地用"人体能量"点

performance art and photography, collaborating with Yann Toma and incorporating the persona of the Man in Gold. A documentary by filmmaker Pawel Kuczynski explores Shusterman's philosophical work and life.

Yann Toma, artist and researcher, received his Ph.D. from the University of Paris 1, Panthéon-Sorbonne, where he directs the Art & Flux laboratory in the ACTE Research Institute. He created the artistic genre of Radiant Flux from which Richard Shusterman's performance art as the Man in Gold emerged. Toma's explorations of light and energy also include a conceptual dimension. He took the defunct Parisian electric company Ouest-Lumière and transformed it into a corporate-structured art network (with himself as President) that engages in artistic research involving collaboration with industrialists, political theorists, and philosophers. He is also an artist-observer at the UN. In December 2015 for the COP21 conference, Toma realized *Human Energy*, a monumental artwork with the Eiffel

亮了埃菲尔铁塔。他的艺术是许多著名展馆的主打展品,包括蓬皮杜文化艺术中心。

玛丽特·班蒂·诺尔海姆,1960年生于挪威,现在丹麦居住和工作。她在伦敦皇家艺术学院获研究生文凭,目前为奥尔堡大学的外聘讲师,讲授艺术。在她艺术观念的构成中,流动性、灵活性、社会参与、直接介入和协作,是为关键要素。诺尔海姆的作品广被展览,他接受许多国家公开委托,创作艺术作品。挪威当代艺术博物馆和丹麦新嘉士伯基金会都收藏有她的作品。她与奥尔胡斯(2017年欧洲文化之都)合作,以钢筋水泥为材料,完成了大型航海雕塑作品《生命舟

Tower. His art is featured in many collections, including the Pompidou Center's.

For more information:
www.ouest-lumiere.org

Marit Benthe Norheim was born in 1960 in Norway and currently lives and works in Denmark. She has a postgraduate diploma from the Royal Academy of Art, London, and is external lecturer in art at Aalborg University. Mobility, flexibility, social participation, direct involvement and collaborations are substantial components in her construction of artistic concepts. Norheim has exhibited widely and has created publicly commissioned artworks in many countries. Her works have been acquired by The Contemporary Art Museum of Norway and the New Carlsberg Foundation in Denmark. She has recently completed a large sailing sculptural project in the medium of concrete. This work, Life-boats (in collaboration with the

楫》，于2016年下水。这些满载着期望、生命和记忆的女性雕像船只，在2017年由船长和船员驾驶，电力引擎驱动，远航欧洲水道，以促进艺术与文化的交流和对话。

克劳斯·安托夫特，1959年生于丹麦，曾在冰岛学习雕塑一年，之后求学于丹麦菲英美术学院。安托夫特专事公共空间雕塑，将周围空间与建筑元素密切联系。他使用的主要材料是花岗石，继承了斯堪的纳维亚半岛石雕传统的遗风。过去35年里，他形成了自己的雕塑语言，着意表达一种存在心理学。

European Capital of Culture, Aarhus 2017) was first launched in Aalborg in 2016. The female sculpture ships (loaded with Longing, Life, and Memories) sailed with captains and crew, propelled forward by electrical engines on the waterways of Europe in 2017 to promote artistic and cultural exchange and dialogue.

For more information:
www.norheim.dk
www.life-boats.com

Claus Ørntoft was born in 1959 in Denmark and attended the Fine Art Academy of Fyn, Denmark, after a year in Iceland as a student of a sculptor there. Ørntoft works primarily with sculptures for public spaces and relates strongly to the spatial and architectural elements in the surroundings. His main material is granite, related to the Nordic tradition of stone carving. During the last 35 years, he has developed his own language of sculpted creatures expressing an existential psychology.

受丹麦艺术基金会和新嘉士伯基金会等委托，安托夫特为丹麦、挪威、格陵兰和冰岛的许多场所做过雕塑，并获得数种丹麦荣誉奖。2012年，他完成了丹麦女王的专项委托，为马赛里斯堡城堡制作雕像。

Ørntoft's works have been created for sites in Denmark, Norway, Greenland and Iceland, commissioned by (among others) the Danish Arts Foundation and the New Carlsberg Foundation, and he has received several Danish honorary prizes. In 2012 he finished a substantial commission for the Queen of Denmark, for Marselisborg Castle.

For more information:
www. Ørntoft.dk

致 谢

ACKNOWLEDGMENTS

致谢 ACKNOWLEDGMENTS

本书问世，要感谢我才思敏捷的许多热心肠朋友和同事，他们不但给我鼓励，而且重塑了我的作品。显而易见，本书所欠情分最多的，是艺术家扬·托马。他生龙活虎地用视觉戏法，将我化身成为金衣人，这样一种变形，其意义远超过了我个人的表演。玛丽特·班蒂·诺尔海姆和克劳斯·安托夫特不但在他们斯坦歇得温馨迷人的家和工作室里优雅地接待了我，而且慷慨相助，允许我和扬使用他们的作品，用于我们自己的创作。我希望本书证明，他们别开生面的盛情招待是多么鼓舞人心。艾尔丝·玛丽·布克达尔和斯达尔·斯坦丝丽两位学者最早邀请我访问奥尔堡大学，感谢前系主任珑·迪尔金科·霍尔姆菲尔德的支持，他安排我做访问教授，参与该系的艺术与技术计划。该计划的研究生赞恩·塞皮纳设计了本书

This book owes its existence to the warm-hearted, creative spirit of friends and colleagues who have both encouraged and reshaped my work. The book's deepest, most obvious debt is to the artist Yann Toma. His irrepressible energy and visionary magic empowered my transfiguration into the Man in Gold, a metamorphosis whose transformational consequences go far beyond my performances in that persona. Marit Benthe Norheim and Claus Ørntoft not only graciously hosted my visits to their enchanting Stenshede home and studios, but also generously allowed Yann and me to use their artworks to create our own. I hope this book testifies to the inspirational power of their affectionate and inventive energy. Else Marie Bukdahl and Stahl Stenslie were the scholars who first brought me to Aalborg University and, with the support of former Dean Lone Dirckinck-Holmfeld, arranged my Visiting Professorship in its Art and Technology Program. One of its graduates, Zane Cerpina, did the graphic formatting of this book.

的图形样式。巴黎的一位文学朋友托马斯·蒙德梅,起草了本书的法文翻译。

感谢两笔基金对本项目的慷慨援助。奥贝尔家族基金会资助我在奥尔堡大学做客座教授,《身体美学杂志》资助了本书的印刷开支。我还衷心感谢施密特家族基金会资助我在佛罗里达亚特兰大大学的职位,让我腾出身来,出外旅行,体验像金衣人这般的历险故事,并得到了佛罗里达亚特兰大大学我的院长希瑟·科尔特曼的热情鼓励。

Thomas Mondemé, a literary friend from Paris, prepared the French translation.

Two foundations deserve thanks for generously supporting this project. The Obel Family Foundation, which sponsored my guest-professor visits to Aalborg and *The Journal of Somaesthetics*, has financed the printing of this book. I also gratefully acknowledge the Schmidt Family Foundation that endows my chair at Florida Atlantic University, giving me the freedom to travel and to experiment with adventurous projects like the Man in Gold, which my FAU Dean, Heather Coltman, has enthusiastically encouraged.